# THE HOLISTIC DOG BLUEPRINT

## Transform Your Dog's Life Through Holistic Care

### Vanessa Richie

LP Media Inc. Publishing
Text copyright © 2025 by LP Media Inc.
All rights reserved.

Publication Data

Vanessa Richie
The Holistic Dog Blueprint — First edition.
Summary: "This comprehensive guide empowers dog owners with natural, science-backed approaches to holistic canine care. Covering nutrition, preventative health, alternative therapies, and emotional well-being, it provides a blueprint for optimizing your dog's health and longevity through balanced, integrative methods"
Provided by publisher.
ISBN: 978-1-961846-14-2
[1. The Holistic Dog Blueprint — Non-Fiction] I. Title.

First paperback edition, 2025

# Table of Contents

# Foreword

When embarking on a journey to provide your dog with the best possible care, it's easy to become overwhelmed by the wealth of information available. This book is designed to be your guide, breaking down the essentials of holistic dog care into five carefully structured sections. Each section builds upon the previous one, creating a comprehensive resource that will help you care for your canine companion in every way.

## Section 1: Foundation

This section lays the groundwork for understanding holistic dog care. It begins by introducing the principles of a holistic approach, exploring how focusing on the body, mind, and spirit can benefit your dog's overall well-being. You'll learn about the importance of nutrition, including how to choose or prepare food that meets your dog's dietary needs while avoiding harmful ingredients. For instance, we discuss the risks associated with processed dog food and provide alternatives for creating a more natural, balanced diet. By the end of this section, you'll have a firm grasp of what holistic care entails and why it's a game-changer for your dog's health.

## Section 2: Environment and Daily Care

A nurturing environment is key to your dog's happiness and safety. In this section, we explore how to create a secure and stimulating home for your pet. You'll find tips on dog-proofing your house, choosing the best bedding and toys, and even teaching children to interact respectfully with your dog. For example, we provide step-by-step instructions for setting up a safe yard that prevents escape while offering shade and comfort. You'll also learn about daily habits like grooming, bathing, and performing health checks to ensure your dog is thriving.

## Section 3: Training and Activities

Physical and mental stimulation are essential to a dog's well-being, and this section dives into how to provide both. We cover topics such as socialization, obedience training, and fun activities tailored to your dog's needs and personality. Whether you're looking to teach basic commands, explore agility training, or simply find ways to keep your dog entertained indoors, this section has you covered. For instance, you'll discover creative ways to turn everyday interactions into opportunities for bonding and learning.

## Section 4: Health and Wellness

A holistic approach to health goes beyond treating illnesses; it's about prevention and maintaining overall balance. This section addresses everything from mental and emotional health to alternative therapies and managing chronic conditions. Learn how to recognize stress signals in your dog and alleviate anxiety, explore the benefits of herbal supplements, and understand when and how to integrate traditional veterinary care with holistic treatments. With practical advice on preventing common ailments and promoting long-term wellness, this section ensures you're prepared to care for your dog in a way that's both effective and compassionate.

## Section 5: Practical Extras

The final section provides hands-on resources to simplify your journey. You'll find recipes for homemade dog food and treats, suggestions for indoor and outdoor activities to keep your dog active, and other helpful tools to enhance your daily routines. For example, we include easy-to-follow recipes that align with a holistic diet, ensuring your dog gets the nutrients they need while enjoying a variety of flavors.

Together, these five sections form a complete guide to holistic dog care, blending practical advice with thoughtful insights to help you meet your dog's needs on every level. By approaching care with a holistic mindset, you'll not only improve your dog's quality of life but also strengthen the bond between you and your furry companion. Let's begin this rewarding journey together.

# Section 1
# FOUNDATION

# CHAPTER 1

# A Holistic Life for Your Dog

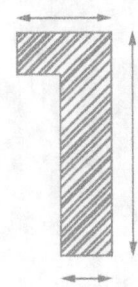

The idea of focusing on all aspects of health—not just one—isn't new. This holistic approach has been around since ancient Greece. What's becoming clearer now is that we should extend this same mindset to the care we give our pets. Sure, we can't address their mental health in exactly the same ways we do for humans, but it's evident that a holistic view is crucial when caring for our furry companions. If you've ever had a pet with separation anxiety, you know that mental well-being is a significant part of an animal's health.

When we bring dogs into our homes, we often think about their diet, training, and exercise needs. However, there's much more to consider to ensure your canine friend is truly happy and healthy. It's about looking at the whole picture—physical, mental, and emotional—to provide the best care possible.

## My Path

When I was a child, my parents brought home our first pet—a sweet mutt we named Benjie, after the popular dog from the 1980s movie (although we spelled his name slightly differently!). We adored him and played with him often, but my parents didn't know much about caring for a dog. He lived outside, chained in an area where we'd spend time with him. Back then, that was normal for dogs: they belonged outside, while cats were the ones kept indoors.

Things have changed a lot since then. We realized dogs were happier inside, so my family started letting our dogs live in the house, though they weren't allowed on the couch. Being a large family of six, we almost always adopted mutts; getting an expensive purebred dog wasn't practical. We also discovered that dogs did better with a buddy, so we often had two dogs at a time.

Over the years, having so many dogs of different breeds and sizes taught us a lot about their various needs. My poor parents ended up with a menagerie of pets. We almost always had at least one dog, but over 18 years, we also cared for cats, gerbils, rabbits, guinea pigs, hamsters, various lizards, and even a mouse.

When I moved out on my own, I realized that being an adult meant I could care for dogs the way I felt was best. No one would undermine my rules unless I did it myself. I could let dogs on the furniture, share some of my food with them, and take them to different places to hike and exercise.

Over four decades as an ardent dog enthusiast, I've learned a lot about dogs that people didn't realize back in the 1980s. My knowledge deepened when I began writing books about different dog breeds. The more I learned, the more I adjusted how I cared for my own dog.

Currently, I have a large Lab/German Shepherd mix who is the most Velcro dog I've ever had. He hates being alone as much as I hate not having a dog nearby. I got him when he was still a puppy—a mature, already house-trained one at about a year and a half old—and I embraced a more natural approach to training and exercise. Even at seven years old, he has lots of energy, which is why I start each day with a walk that lasts between an hour and a half and two hours.

Being such a Velcro dog, praise is almost as effective as treats—though with a Lab mix, treats always work, no matter how much he's eaten! With so many different dog breeds and personalities in my life, I've learned to take a holistic approach to ensure my dogs live as long and happy a life as possible.

## From Wolves to Pets: The Fascinating Story of Humans and Dogs

There is a good reason why dogs are called man's best friend. DNA testing and studies conducted over the last five years have shown that dogs have been our companions longer than any other creature. Domestication likely started around 33,000 years ago, and there is plenty of evidence that 15,000 years ago, dogs were already a part of human civilizations. Since those early days of domestication, the roles of dogs have significantly changed, with a lot of that shift happening over the last five centuries. Originally, they were companions that helped humans survive and hunt. As humans became more adept in both of these areas, especially after they began to settle down and farm, they realized that dogs were incredibly versatile when it came to the kinds of tasks they could do.

Wealthy people and royalty have had canines for pets for a very long time, but over the last century or two, a growing number of people started to adopt dogs just to have them around as pets. The dogs weren't expected to do much, if any, work. Instead, they started becoming a regular part of people's homes, including those who weren't wealthy or royal. Even in homes where dogs worked some of the day, they were treated with more affection.

Today, the vast majority of dogs are pets. Even those who work jobs are treated like pets after hours. You see police adopting their K9 companions when the dog reaches retirement age, ranchers filming their collies herding sheep (and then spoiling those collies), and dogs offering emotional support to trauma victims. We've even created the unique position of emotional support animals, which dogs often fill.

Just having a pet around can help to improve your health. It's a unique symbiotic relationship that allows dogs to relax in the security of your pack while giving you all the health benefits of having a loving companion. They even provide a holistic approach to your health, dragging you outside to exercise, providing emotional support when you're stressed or upset, and keeping you from getting lonely.

## Natural Approach for People

A holistic approach to health may be thousands of years old, but people have become disconnected from those early roots, believing they can treat different problems individually. That has not been effective. There is a greater need for a holistic approach to our health today because there are more chemicals and pollutants that are harming us. The symptoms of this problem are very obvious because of the rise in obesity and chronic ailments, largely caused by highly processed foods that are high in preservatives and sugars. We don't move around enough to offset the calories we eat, which causes additional problems. Stress levels are far too high, creating a whole different set of health problems. Anxiety and depression are common issues that have only recently become something that people realize shouldn't just be

"shaken off" because they are signs of a deeper issue.

As people become less satisfied with their lives and their health suffers, they have started looking for more traditional ways of getting healthy, and that has led to the return to traditional holistic methods.

## The Reason This Approach Applies to Pets

People are more likely to look for a more natural treatment for their pets when traditional treatments aren't successful (which mirrors how they tend to manage their own health). Dogs can very much benefit from you adopting a more holistic life. The odds are that if you are eating more processed food, you are also feeding your dog highly processed food. If you don't get enough exercise, your dog probably doesn't either. If you don't manage your emotions effectively, it's going to affect your dog because canines are much more attuned to emotions than people are.

Just like you should consult a physician as you start to make changes to your life, you should consult your vet as you start to make changes to how you care for your dog. Your dog isn't going to be able to tell you if he's having trouble with a change in diet, so your vet can tell you what to look for as you adjust your pet's meals.

## A Reason to Get Excited

We already don't get long enough with our canine companions, so any change that is likely to extend and improve the quality of their lives is more than worth it. People who have switched to a more holistic approach report feeling much better physically, mentally, and emotionally. You can give your dog a similar sense of improvement, giving back some of the same unconditional love he gives you.

# CHAPTER 2

# Holistic — What Does It Mean?

It's important to remember that holistic health care is as much about maintaining healthy habits as it is treating current issues. After all, if you can do more now to reduce things like your dog's stress, you will reduce his health risks later.

## Definition of Holistic

A holistic approach utilizes both Western and Eastern medicine. Unlike more modern methods, holistic health care considers the person or dog as a whole and not just individual parts. For example, if your dog breaks a leg, the common modern-day approach is to simply treat the broken leg. A better way of helping the dog during the healing process is to treat the dog's body, mind, emotions, and spirit. When a dog breaks a leg, it affects all aspects of the animal's life. An injury can be emotionally devastating, especially if it will affect the dog's life going forward, such as impacting his ability to be active. This can leave a dog feeling depression, anxiety, or other mental conditions that are related to trauma and stress. Spiritually, the dog probably feels low or upset.

Maintaining a healthy lifestyle goes beyond just taking care of the body. There is a notion out there that a holistic approach to health is mystical and bizarre. People tend to be under the impression that they need to burn incense or sage, sleep surrounded by crystals, and avoid hygienic products.

These are entirely wrong impressions. Can you do those things? Sure, if that's something you are interested in, but that's not holistic health care. Nor does being holistic mean going vegan and avoiding all your favorite foods or forcing that kind of lifestyle on your dog. It's not exercising vigorously for two hours a day and taking up tai chi—unless you enjoy that kind of activity.

Living holistically simply means treating every aspect of yourself and your dog, not just one part. Your mind, body, emotions, and spirit are all critical parts of who you are, and when one of these is unwell, all of them will be affected. That is also true of your dog.

## Using Stress to Understand Overall Effects

According to the American Institute of Stress:

Stress in the US is estimated to be

**20%**
**higher**

than the international average.

Roughly

**55%**

of Americans report stress on a daily basis.

Of the people who completed a stress survey,

**57%**

said they felt stress at a level that left them paralyzed.

**63%**

of Americans said high levels of work stress have made them consider quitting their job.

Stress isn't an obvious physical ailment, but there are clear physical signs. Short-term stress causes things like tension and shallow breathing. Long-term stress is more detrimental, causing sustained muscle tension (resulting in headaches and migraines), difficulty sleeping, digestive issues, weight loss or gain, and high blood pressure. These problems contribute to much more serious issues, such as heart disease, heart attacks, strokes, and cancer.

## A New Way to Look at Health Care

Health care has four components:

1. Promoting good health means practicing healthy habits and maintaining good health.

2. Palliation is managing symptoms when you have been diagnosed with an ailment.

3. Suppression occurs when a person is successfully treated for an ailment, but they are less healthy than they were prior to becoming ill.

4. Being cured means the illness has been treated, all the symptoms disappear, and the person is at least as healthy as they were prior to the illness.

Returning to our earlier example of a broken limb, if that happened in a car accident, the person might develop a fear of being in cars, creating distress that keeps them from returning to the life they had prior to the accident. Ignoring any one part of your health is going to be less successful than if you treat all four parts to make sure you heal.

For much of the last century, Western medicine has focused solely on disease and physical treatment, ignoring all other aspects of the problem. The result is a lot of pills, surgeries, and radiation. The focus is on reacting to problems and then treating them instead of taking preventative steps to keep a person from getting sick. There are some medical professionals who do offer preventative measures for things like obesity and other conditions, but often, this only happens after a more significant problem is found.

Health care includes a lot more beyond illness, though. Instead of focusing on one aspect, you should work to improve your health by looking at the big picture. This applies to dogs as well. Take a big-picture approach to your dog's health, and your furry companion is much more likely to live a longer, healthier, happier life.

## Common Causes for Ailments in Dogs and What Vets Do and Don't Say

Like humans, dogs suffer from a lot of common ailments, many of which aren't life threatening. They have allergies, arthritis, and infections. They also have issues that people are less likely to have, such as hip dysplasia, heartworms, and other types of parasites. Most of these are treated through medication and not much else.

Allergies and skin conditions are common for a vast majority of dog breeds. Often, the recommendation is to apply ointment or some other medicine to the problem, along with a cone or other device to keep your dog from licking the medicine. This can alleviate some of your dog's discomfort, but it is essentially just a palliative treatment, and it often does not take care of the problem. You'll have to apply that medicine again in the near future to keep the discomfort to a minimum.

Even more problematic is the fact that a lot of medicines have steroids, which can adversely affect other parts of your dog. The symptom may be treated, but the reason your dog has a hot spot is because the body is trying to remove toxins, such as allergens, and the medication is actively blocking his body's ability to do that. As a result, the toxin may seep into other organs, creating a much more serious condition.

When toxins can't leave through the skin, they may enter the lungs, causing asthma, bronchitis, or chronic respiratory infections, or the toxins may enter the dog's digestive tract, resulting in bowel inflammation, diarrhea, vomiting, and numerous diseases (including cancer). At the same time, the medication suppresses the dog's immune system, causing stress on the kidneys and liver. A relatively minor problem could then become significant because the treatment focused only on treating the symptom.

## Holistic Care for Pets

Taking a holistic approach to your dog's health care means you are tending to his body, mind, emotions, and spirit. Some of these aspects are a little harder to notice in dogs because they don't communicate in as clear a way as people do. The hardest thing to notice is their spirit because they don't talk. There are numerous examples of dogs feeling heartbroken over the loss of their person or companion. Perhaps the most famous is Hachiko, an Akita who never stopped waiting for his person to return from the train station for years after the man died.

There are many components to establishing a healthy lifestyle for your dog:

- Nutrition
- Physical environment
- Physical activity
- Socialization
- Training
- Mental health
- Emotional health
- Herbs and supplements
- Alternative therapies
- Disease and medications

The last three can have an integrated approach, using traditional techniques and newer medications.

CHAPTER 3
# Nutrition

Your dog's diet is the number one consideration when it comes to his health.

What your dog eats is foundational—if you feed him too much, too little, or unhealthy food on a regular basis, it will adversely affect his health, no matter what else you do right. This extends to eating homemade food. You can mix the food you make for your dog with kibble or other processed foods, but making sure you feed your dog fresh food is the best way to improve his diet. Sure, it may take a little more time, but you can use a lot of the same foods in your dog's meals as you do your own. It's not a matter of cooking an entirely different meal but making sure you don't include things in your dog's food that are potentially dangerous to his health.

## Traditional Attitudes about Dog Food

A few decades ago, the attitude toward feeding pets was similar to feeding children and adults. As long as it was edible, it should be fine. When people realized that processed foods weren't providing all the essential nutrients their bodies needed, they started taking dietary supplements to fill the gaps. These supplements—like vitamins, minerals, and herbal extracts—helped ensure they were getting the nutrients necessary for good health. Soon enough, pet owners wondered if their dogs might be missing out too. So, they began giving their dogs supplements to support their pets' health, recognizing that commercial dog food might not cover all their nutritional needs.

It was really only toward the end of the twentieth century and the early part of the twenty-first century when people started to realize that highly processed food was a large part of the problem. The way the food was processed removed a lot of the nutritional value. This applies to dog food, too, which has been far less regulated than food for people.

Perhaps the worst attitude toward dog food is "it was good enough for my dog growing up" because this means ignoring the studies and findings that now indicate certain foods are not healthy for dogs. Sometimes, this approach is taken because dog food that is better for your dog's health is more expensive. This is an easy sentiment to understand, but it really isn't a good reason to keep feeding your dog food that is unhealthy.

My current dog is a 75-pound Labrador Retriever mix. When he had digestive issues a while back, the vet said we needed to change his diet. Then, he recommended a bag of food that was nearly $100 per 20-pound bag, which wouldn't even get my dog through a full month.

That's when I started to realize that the best way to feed my dog healthy food was to make his meals myself. I can feed him a lot of the same foods that I eat, and we are both much healthier for cutting out the dining out and commercial dog food. Admittedly, I still feed him kibble with each meal, but it isn't the most important part of his meal. It's more of a way of slowing down his eating—as a Lab, he eats too fast when you don't force him to slow down with a Kong or smaller food chunks. I know he gets the necessary nutrition because I make at least half of each of his meals. It's cheaper and healthier, and it really doesn't take that much more time.

# Why a Healthy Diet Is Important for a Dog

The saying "We are what we eat" is just as true for dogs as it is for humans. No matter how active your dog is or isn't, he needs to have a healthy caloric intake to keep from gaining weight.

The following are the most common health problems caused by poor diet:

- Anorexia
- Coat and skin conditions
- Diabetes
- Digestive issues and stomach problems
- Eye issues, including loss of eyesight
- Heart disease
- Kidney disease
- Liver disease
- Obesity
- Pancreatitis
- Periodontal disease
- Reduced immunity
- Weight loss

A poor diet results in a lower quality of life for your dog.

As you probably already know, dogs are largely carnivorous, but a healthy diet for dogs requires more than just protein.

The following table provides the primary nutritional requirements for dogs:

| Nutrient | Sources | Puppy | Adult |
| --- | --- | --- | --- |
| Protein | Meat, eggs, soybeans, corn, wheat, peanut butter | 22% of diet | 18% of diet |
| Fats | Fish oil, flaxseed oil, canola oil, pork fat, poultry fat, safflower oil, sunflower oil, soybean oil | 8% to 15% of diet | 5% to 15% of diet |
| Calcium | Dairy, animal organ tissue, meats, legumes (typically beans) | 1% of diet | 0.6% of diet |
| Phosphorus | Meat and pet supplements | 0.8% of diet | 0.5% of diet |
| Sodium | Meat, eggs | 0.3% of diet | 0.06% of diet |

The following are the remaining nutrients dogs require, all of them less than 1% of a puppy or adult dog diet:

- Arginine
- Histidine
- Isoleucine
- Leucine
- Lysine
- Methionine + cystine
- Phenylalanine + tyrosine
- Threonine
- Tryptophan
- Valine
- Chloride

Most of the primary nutritional needs your dog has can be classified into one of three groups.

- **Proteins and amino acids** — Protein contains the necessary amino acids to produce glucose, which is essential for giving your dog energy. A lack of protein in your dog's diet will result in him being lethargic. His coat may start to look dull, and he is likely to lose weight. Conversely, if your dog gets too much protein, his body will store the excess as fat, and he will gain weight.

- **Fat and fatty acids** — Most fats that your dog needs are found in meat. Seed oils provide a lot of the necessary healthy fats, too, with peanut butter being one of the most common sources. Fats break down into fatty acids, which your dog needs for fat-soluble vitamins that help with regular cell functions. Perhaps the most obvious benefit of fats and fatty acids can be seen in your dog's coat, which will look and feel much healthier when he is getting the right nutrients.

  The following is a list of potential health issues that might arise if your dog does not get adequate fats in his daily diet:

  - His coat will look less healthy.
  - His skin may be dry and itchy.
  - His immune system could be compromised, making it easier for your dog to get sick.
  - He may have an increased risk of heart disease. The primary concern if your dog gets too much fat is that he will become obese, leading to additional health problems.

- **Carbohydrates and cooked foods** — Dogs have been living with humans for millennia, so their dietary needs have evolved like our own. They can eat foods with carbohydrates to supplement the energy typically provided by proteins and fats. If you cook grains (such as barley, corn, and rice) prior to feeding them to your dog, it will be easier for him to digest those complex carbohydrates. Note that if your dog is allergic to grains, potatoes are also high in carbohydrates.

It's best to avoid giving your dog human foods that have a lot of sodium and preservatives.

Water is also essential to keep your dog healthy. Make a habit of checking your dog's water bowl several times a day so he does not get dehydrated.

## A Closer Look at What's in Dog Food

It's difficult to entirely stop using dog food because sometimes you need to be able to feed your pet quickly. With that being the case, you should know what's in commercial dog food:

- **Bone meal** — This includes ground bones that add calcium and phosphorus to your dog's diet. Generally, the source animal for the bones is not specified, so if your dog is allergic or sensitive to any type of meat, you may need to avoid this ingredient.

- **Colostrum** — This is a type of milk produced by dairy cattle; it is lower in lactose than the milk in your refrigerator. It has amino acids, antibodies, minerals, and vitamins. It may affect your dog if he is lactose intolerant.

- **Dairy products** — This is more processed milk, which is higher in lactose. It will almost certainly adversely affect your dog if he is lactose intolerant.

- **Hydrolyzed animal proteins** — These are additives to enhance the flavor of the food. Foods with these additives may help dogs with food allergies to more typical proteins.

- **Egg** — Eggs have a lot of nutritional value for dogs, including being good for their coats. However, a dog with a history of heart issues or high blood pressure should have eggs less often as large amounts can exacerbate these problems.

- **Fish oil** — This is usually made from fish that are high in oil, like mackerel, salmon, sardines, and tuna. It is considered very healthy for dogs and is also a supplement that you can give your dog to improve his health and coat. It's used in the treatment of many health conditions in dogs, such as cardiovascular disease and joint issues.

- **Grains** — The type of grain found in dog food is usually barley, cereals, corn, maize, maize germ, maize gluten, oats, rice, rye, sorghum, spelt, or wheat.

- **Liver** — Often added as a type of meat, liver has a lot of nutritional value for dogs, and it's easy for most dogs to digest.

- **Meats** — The options for meat in dog food are usually beef, chicken, crustaceans, duck, fish, lamb, pork, poultry, rabbit, turkey, and venison.

- **Meat and animal derivatives** — Generally considered filler and junk, these are theoretically animal parts, but it is unclear what kind of meats are included or even what parts. For dogs with sensitive stomachs or allergies, this is an ingredient that should be avoided.

- **Meat meal** — This is a fine, dry powder made out of the parts of animals that people don't eat. It used to be one of the most popular highly processed elements in dog foods, and it can still make up a large part of commercial food. It can be beneficial, but details about what is included in the meal make it a bit harder to trust, especially for dogs with digestive issues.

- **Poultry fat** — This is typically added to foods made with meat meal because the process of making the meal removes most of the healthy fats. It is high in fat, and many dog foods include more of it as a flavoring. While it is fine in moderate amounts, it's unhealthy when used excessively.

- **Specified animal fats and oils** — Similar to meats, these ingredients may include a specified type of animal fats and oil.

- **Specified grain germ** — This is fairly healthy for dogs since it contains non-carb nutrients like unsaturated oils, fatty acids, and vitamins B and E.

- **Tripe** — Made from the stomach of a grazing animal (such as pigs, cows, goats, deer, sheep, and pigs), tripe is considered very nutritious for dogs. Rich in fat and protein, it provides essential oils.

- **Unspecified animal fats** — This ingredient indicates the inclusion of animal fats but doesn't say exactly what the source animals were. It's not a good ingredient for dogs with digestive issues.

- **Wheat feed** — This ingredient is not properly defined so that consumers can know exactly what it is. It is thought to mean parts of wheat that fail to meet the necessary standards for people to eat. Foods that include this ingredient are probably not a good choice for your dog, especially since wheat is already problematic for canines.

Many commercial dog foods contain fillers, which inexpensively increase the amount of food without adding much (or any) nutritional value. The following are the most commonly used fillers:

- Cereals
- Derivatives of vegetable origin
- Maize and maize flour
- Soy
- Wheat
- White potato (yams/sweet potatoes are rich in nutrients) and potato starch
- White rice (brown rice is richer in nutrients) and rice flour

In addition to fillers not having much nutritional value, they tend to be harder on the canine digestive tract. Nor are they likely to make your dog feel full for long, so he will probably get hungry much faster. Considering the mostly empty calories, it's not a good idea to just feed him more.

## New Natural Diet Ideas and Different Types of Diets

There are many different types of diets for dogs, and they can be tailored to every dog's special needs. Natural diets are not the same as organic diets.

- Natural diets refer to meals that are made of natural foods, so they are solely composed of ingredients that are plants or animals. They have not undergone any kind of chemical synthetic processes, and there are no additives or fillers added to the food.
- Organic refers more to the process used to grow the plants or raise the animals that are going to be used in the food. The plants and animals cannot be processed or raised in a way that includes chemicals (no use of chemicals to speed up growth or kill pests with pesticides, and no antibiotics, hormones, or cloning for the animals).

Natural diets focus on one of two primary needs: preventative care for healthy dogs and curative diets to help treat or reverse diseases.

- Preventative diets focus on giving your dog better-quality food to reduce or prevent diseases related to poorer diets.
- Curative diets, also known as therapeutic diets, focus on giving your dog food to manage health issues. These can be used in coordination with other types of treatment.

Both of these types of diets are holistic. If a dog is healthy, a curative diet isn't necessary. If a dog is ill, the dietary focus should be on treating the illness.

I strongly recommend that you at least combine dog food with homemade food as there are benefits for both you and your dog. However, odds are you are going to need dog food sometimes, so it's important to know what to look for and what to avoid when you buy commercial dog foods.

Make sure that you are buying the best dog food you can afford, and always take into account your dog's size, energy level, and age. If you aren't sure which brand of

food is best, talk with a breeder about the foods they recommend. If you didn't use a breeder to find your dog, you can also ask your vet. Even after you start following the recommendations, though, you will need to see how your dog behaves after making the change. Over time, you will probably need to adjust the types of food and nutrients your dog gets because, as canines age, their needs change.

Some dogs may be picky eaters and get tired of repeatedly eating the same food. While you shouldn't frequently change the brand of food because that can upset your dog's stomach, you can get foods that come in assorted flavors. You can also change the taste by adding a bit of wet (canned) food. Adding one-fourth to one-third of a can for each meal is an easy change you can make to ensure your dog's happiness.

For more details on commercial options, check out the website Dog Food Advisor. It provides reviews on various dog food brands, as well as information on recalls and contamination issues.

# Commercial Dry Food

Dry dog food is what most people feed their dogs.

| PROS OF DRY DOG FOOD | CONS OF DRY DOG FOOD |
|---|---|

**PROS OF DRY DOG FOOD**

+ Convenience
+ Variety
+ Availability
+ Affordability
+ Most manufacturers follow nutritional recommendations. (Not all of them do this, so do your brand research before you buy.)
+ Specially formulated for different canine life stages
+ Can be used for training
+ Easy to store

**CONS OF DRY DOG FOOD**

✖ Requires research to ensure you don't buy doggy junk food
✖ Packaging is not always honest
✖ Recalls for food contamination
✖ Loose FDA nutritional regulations
✖ Low-quality food may have questionable ingredients

The convenience and ease on your budget mean you are almost certainly going to buy kibble for your dog. This is perfectly fine, and most dogs will be more than happy to eat kibble. But be sure you know what brand you are feeding your dog, and pay attention to kibble recalls so you can stop feeding your dog a certain brand if necessary. Check out the following sites for recall information:

**Dog Food Recalls**
www.dogfoodadvisor.com

**American Kennel Club**
www.AKC.org

**Dog Food Guide**
www.dogfood.guide

## Commercial Wet Food

Most dogs prefer wet dog food over kibble, but it's more expensive. Wet dog food can be purchased in large packs that are easy to store.

| PROS OF WET DOG FOOD | CONS OF WET DOG FOOD |
|---|---|
| ✚ Helps keep dogs hydrated | ✖ Dog bowls must be washed after every meal |
| ✚ Has a richer scent and flavor | ✖ Can soften bowel movements |
| ✚ Easier to eat for dogs with dental problems (particularly those with missing teeth) or for dogs that have been ill | ✖ Can be messier than kibble |
| ✚ Convenient and easy to serve | ✖ Once opened, it has a short shelf-life and should be covered and refrigerated |
| ✚ Unopened, it can last between one and three years | ✖ More expensive than dry dog food and comes in small quantities |
| ✚ Nutritionally balanced based on current pet nutrition recommendations | ✖ Packaging is not always honest |
| | ✖ Recalls for food contamination |
| | ✖ Loose FDA regulations |

Like dry dog food, wet dog food is convenient, and picky dogs are much more likely to eat it than kibble. If your dog gets sick, use wet dog food to ensure that he is still eating and gets the necessary nutrition each day. It may be harder to switch back to kibble once your dog is healthy, but you can always add a little wet food to make each meal more appetizing.

## Variety in Foods

Just like you have some variation in your diet, eating something different for breakfast than you eat for dinner—give your dog a variety of foods. You will need to be careful in how you introduce new foods, as making a significant change can cause diarrhea or other digestive issues.

This is why making your dog's meals at least partly homemade can be incredibly beneficial. You don't have to change the kibble or wet dog food very often (although it is pretty easy to have a few different types of wet dog food readily available) since you can regularly offer your dog a more varied diet.

## Dangerous Dog Foods

Before we get into cooking for your dog, it's important to understand that not all foods you can eat are safe for dogs. Probably the most famous example is chocolate. When you eat chocolate, your biggest concern is generally the sugar content. For dogs, chocolate can be deadly because of the way their body processes it.

The following is a list of foods you should **NEVER** feed your dog:

- Apple seeds
- Chocolate
- Coffee
- Cooked bones (They can kill a dog when the bones splinter in his mouth or stomach.)
- Corn on the cob (The cob is deadly to dogs; corn off the cob is fine.)
- Grapes/raisins
- Macadamia nuts
- Onions and chives
- Peaches, persimmons, and plums
- Tobacco (Your dog will not realize it's not a food and may eat it if it's left out.)
- Xylitol (a sugar substitute in candies and baked goods)
- Yeast

In addition to this list, consult the Canine Journal website for a lengthy list of other foods that are dangerous to dogs.

## Feeding Schedules and Food Amounts

There are so many factors to consider when feeding your dog, such as breed, size, activity level, health, and age, that it can be overwhelming when you get your first dog. Then, you have to remember to adjust your dog's diet over time, especially when a dog reaches his senior years.

Since dogs are pack animals, whenever you eat a meal, your dog should be eating too. Break up his caloric intake over two or three meals a day. For example, I only eat two meals a day, so my family (dog included!) eats both meals together. Since I walk my dog for an hour and a half to two hours in the morning, we tend to have a larger breakfast after the walk. Then we have a smaller dinner, followed by a half-hour evening stroll. We feed him less now since he is an aging adult dog. In a couple more years, we'll adjust his food again since seniors don't need as much food.

Let's take a look at the elements that most affect how much you should feed your dog.

## Size/Weight

When it comes to feeding dogs, we usually refer to their weight to indicate how large they are. However, this refers to the weight they should be. If your dog is either overweight or underweight, talk with your vet to determine what your pup's caloric intake should be.

The following chart is based on a healthy weight for an adult dog.

| Dog Size | Calories per day |
| --- | --- |
| 10 lbs. | 420 during hot months<br>630 during cold months |
| 20 lbs. | 700 during hot months<br>1,050 during cold months |
| 30 lbs. | 900 during hot months<br>1,400 during cold months |
| 50 lbs. | 1,350 during hot months<br>2,000 during cold months |
| 70–100 lbs. | 1,680 during hot months<br>2,500 during cold months |
| 100+ lbs. | 2,400 during hot months<br>3,600 during cold months |

If your dog is fixed, he needs fewer calories than an intact dog. You should talk to your vet, but usually, fixed dogs need about 85% of the calories of a dog who hasn't been spayed or neutered.

30

# Age

Your dog's age is another major factor you should consider when calculating how much food he needs to be healthy.

### PUPPY FOOD

During the first 12 months of their lives, puppies need more calories and have different nutritional needs to promote growth, so feed them a food made specifically for puppies. Puppies can have up to four meals a day. Just be careful not to overfeed them, particularly if you use treats during training.

Since your dog's breed is a significant factor in determining how much your puppy will grow, you need to talk to your vet during each visit to make sure that your puppy is growing at the expected rate. This is the best way to ensure your dog is eating well. A Great Dane puppy is going to need a lot more than a Chihuahua puppy. Make sure to discuss this aspect during each vet visit to ensure your puppy is getting the right amount of food.

### ADULT DOG FOOD

The primary difference between puppy food and adult dog food is puppy food is higher in calories and nutrients. Dog food manufacturers reduce these nutrients in adult dog food, as adults no longer need lots of calories to sustain growth. As a rule, when a canine reaches about 90% of his predicted adult size, you should switch him to an adult dog food.

It is also recommended that you set the food and water bowls at an elevated level so your dog doesn't have to lean over so far to eat. This isn't much of a problem for smaller dogs, but the larger your dog, the higher you should raise his bowl to help him eat more comfortably. This can help reduce the risk of bloat as well for breeds that are prone to it. If you notice your dog eating too quickly, consider getting a dog feeder that limits how quickly he can eat. After 15 minutes, pick up the food bowl so that he does not continuously eat over the course of the day. However, always leave fresh water out for him, making it easily accessible all day and night.

### SENIOR DOG FOOD

Senior dogs are not always capable of being as active as they were in their younger days. If you notice your dog is slowing down, suffers joint pain, and shows a lack of stamina when taking long walks, you can assume he is entering his senior years. Consult with your vet if you think it's time to change the type of food you feed your dog.

The primary difference between adult and senior dog food is senior dog food contains less fat and more antioxidants to help fight weight gain. Senior dogs also need more protein, which will probably make your dog happy because that usually means more meat. Protein helps to maintain your dog's aging muscles. He should also be eating less phosphorus during his golden years to avoid the risk of developing hyperphosphatemia. This is a condition where dogs have excessive amounts of phosphorus in their bloodstream, and older dogs are at greater risk of developing it. The level of phosphorus in the body is controlled by the kidneys; as such, elevated levels of phosphorus are usually an indication of a problem with the kidneys.

Senior dog food has the correct number of calories for reduced activity, which means no adjustment of quantity is needed unless you notice weight gain. Consult your vet if you notice your dog is putting on weight because this could be a sign of illness.

## ACTIVITY LEVEL

Activity levels are another important consideration for your dog.

The following table defines activity levels based on how much time a dog is active. However, keep in mind that this does not reflect how vigorous the exercise is. If you jog for 30 minutes, that's moderate activity. If you walk slowly with a lot of stopping and talking for an hour, that's low activity.

| Activity Level | Daily Duration of Activity |
| --- | --- |
| Sedentary | Less than 30 minutes |
| Low activity | Between 30 and 60 minutes |
| Moderate activity | 1 to 2 hours |
| High activity | 2 to 3 hours |
| Working and performance | Over three hours |

## Treats!

If you have a dog, you have to have treats. This is one of the best ways of training a pet because most dogs respond well to extra food. Puppies, in particular, require treats because they aren't old enough to understand much beyond treats as an incentive. You should switch over to praise as early as possible as an incentive because treats tend to be much higher in calories.

Even when you don't need to train your dog, treats are a nice thing to have on hand. They're like doggy desserts. We have treats for our boy that help to keep him mentally stimulated—one of his favorite games is finding the treasure. We take a few dry treats and hide them in a couple of his blankets. He then proceeds to dig through the blankets, rooting out and scarfing down the treats. We use two blankets to hide five or six treats because that will keep him happily occupied for five minutes or so, giving us enough time to enjoy our dessert while he has his.

It is admittedly much harder to make treats for dogs than to buy them. Fortunately, there are some treats that are beneficial in other ways. Some of our favorites are dental dog treats and rawhide sticks. Both of these take more time for our dog to eat, and they help to keep his teeth a bit cleaner. He does still need to have his teeth brushed regularly, but it's just one more way to help keep his teeth looking amazing.

Finally, you need to consider treats as a part of your dog's daily caloric intake. They aren't calorie free, so you need to give your dog a bit less food depending on how many treats he gets, just like you might eat a bit less of your dinner so that you have room for dessert. Dogs don't tend to pay attention to if they are full, and they will eat treats even if they aren't hungry, so you need to make sure you keep them from overindulging.

If you are interested in making your own treats, the Appendix includes a few recipes.


## Special Diets for Special Needs

Some breeds are prone to digestive issues. Other dogs have allergies, and some dogs need special diets because of an illness. Your dog's diet depends on his unique needs. Even allergies don't have a single diet solution because there are so many types of allergies. For example, my dog has a problem eating chicken. Since my family eats only chicken, turkey, and fish for meat, we have to make adjustments for his food when we eat chicken. Generally, I give him some of the same fruits and veggies we are eating but add different meat to his meal (like tuna—he responds like a cat to the sound of a can opener). Sometimes, we save some of the egg or turkey bacon from breakfast and add that to his meal. Leftovers make great dog meals; the food does not go to waste, and he gets to feel like he's eating the same thing as his people.

You will need to talk to your vet about what kind of food your dog should be eating, especially if he has a more serious illness, such as kidney, heart, or liver issues. Again, your dog's activity level and age are other important factors that determine what he should be eating.

If you plan to make your dog's food and you have dietary restrictions, you will need to make sure your dog's nutritional needs are met. That means you will need to do a lot of research and have some long conversations with your vet to make sure your dog doesn't suffer.

For example, meat is the best source of protein for your dog. If you plan to feed him a vegetarian diet, it is very important that you talk to your vet first. It's incredibly difficult to ensure that a carnivore receives adequate protein while on a vegetarian diet. Puppies, in particular, need to have adequate protein to become healthy adults, so you may need to give your puppy a diet with meat and then switch to a vegetarian diet after your canine becomes an adult.

## A More Cost-Effective and Environmentally Responsible Way to Feed Your Dog

To give your dog the healthiest diet, it's best to make at least part (if not all) of his meals. It's not only healthier for your dog, but it is considerably cheaper than the lowest-cost dog food. You can control how healthy your dog's meals are, and it also tends to have the added benefit of getting you to eat healthier.

The last significant benefit (if those aren't enough) is that it's environmentally more responsible. You want to encourage more responsible farming and animal treatment, and it's much easier to see how the food and animals were treated when you work with human food instead of dog food. Taking better care of your dog, eating better yourself, and benefiting the planet is the best approach to taking care of your dog. After all, part of a holistic approach includes your dog's surroundings, and he needs a healthy outdoor environment.

# ENVIRONMENT AND DAILY CARE

# CHAPTER 4

# Physical Environment

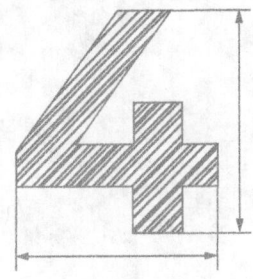

You want to live in a place that suits your preferences—and so does your dog. From minimizing dangers to setting up a comfortable environment, there is a lot you can do to give your pet the right kind of home setting. Some things are fairly obvious, such as making sure your dog has a space that meets his needs. For example, if you have a Great Dane, he needs a bigger sleeping space. If you have a Husky, you need a larger yard.

Fortunately, dogs are a lot easier to please than people. Once you set up your dog's space and prepare your home and yard for him, you won't have to do nearly as much to keep your new pet happy and safe. Sure, your pup will need a new bed every so often, and you will need to buy new toys periodically. You may also need to replace your dog's bowls (especially if you bring a puppy into your home—he will almost certainly chew on the bowl). Still, it is far easier to update and refresh your dog's stuff than your own. A dog bed and bowls cost much less and are easier to find than a new human bed or dishes for yourself.

This chapter goes through the many different aspects of providing a holistic environment for your dog. Some of them will be obvious, and some will give you something new to consider.

## Creating a Safe Home

Keeping your dog safe is your priority. You have to make sure all chemicals in and around your home are secure so your dog can't accidentally drink antifreeze or any other chemicals. There are foods and plants that could be dangerous to your dog as well, and these will also need to be secured so that he cannot get to them. For example, if you grow things like onions or grapes, those are toxic to dogs, so you will need to block off those spaces.

The most dangerous rooms and items in your home will be just as hazardous to your puppy as if he were an infant or toddler. Some adult dogs require the same kind of puppy-proofing you need to implement with an actual puppy; that's just the nature of some breeds and personalities. Higher-energy dogs or ones that tend to suffer from anxiety are much more likely to get into dangerous situations if you don't eliminate all the hazards before their arrival. Be aware that puppies will try to eat virtually anything! Anything within reach is considered fair game to a teething puppy. This can be true for adult dogs, too, but clearly, their reach will be a lot higher off the ground, including in your kitchen. If your adult dog has not been taught not to chew on items, you are going to need to do a lot more to secure the things around your home. Keep this in mind as you go about dog-proofing your home.

The first thing to do is to post your vet's number on the fridge and in at least one other room in the house, as well as program it into your phone. Family members or dog sitters need to know who to call in case of an emergency.

## Plant Dangers

To protect your dog, you need to learn about all the greenery both inside and outside your home to make sure he doesn't try to supplement those healthy, holistic meals with some fresh plants that could be harmful.

| Mildly Toxic | Mildly to Moderately Toxic | Moderately Toxic | Moderately to Highly Toxic | Highly Toxic |
|---|---|---|---|---|
| Asparagus Fern | Aloe | Alocasia | Cactus | Brunfelsia |
| Begonia | Amaryllis | Arrowhead | Kalanchoe | Desert Rose |
| Ficus Benjamina | Calla Lily | Dieffenbachia | | Flame Lily |
| Flamingo Flower | Cyclamen | Dracaena Fragrans | | Kaffir Lily |
| Gardenia | Dracaena | English Ivy | | Oleander |
| Geranium | Philodendron | Eucalyptus | | Sago Palm |
| Golden Pothos | | Peyote | | Bird of Paradise (Strelitzia) |
| Jade Plant | | | | |
| Schefflera | | | | |
| Ti Plant | | | | |
| ZZ Plant | | | | |

## Indoor Hazards and Fixes

If you are introducing a dog to your home, you need to expect some level of exploration, and that means making sure that all potential hazards are removed or made inaccessible.

The best way to assess your home is to get on your hands and knees to view each room from your dog's perspective prior to his arrival. Regardless of the breed and size, you will need to check both low and high spots. For example, Corgis and Shiba Inu are small but incredibly intelligent—and they have been known to move furniture to gain access to places that should be out of reach.

| Hazards | Fixes | Time Estimate |
|---|---|---|
| **KITCHEN** | | |
| Poisons | Keep in secure, childproof cabinets or on high shelves. | 30 min. |
| Trash Cans | Use a lockable trash can or keep it in a secure location. | 10 min. |
| Appliances | Make sure all cords are out of reach. | 15 min. |
| Human Food | Keep out of reach. | Constant (Start making it a habit!) |
| **FLOORS** | | |
| Slippery Surfaces | Put down rugs or special mats designed to stick to the floor. | 30 min.–1 hour |
| Training Area | Train your dog on nonslip surfaces. | Constant |
| **BATHROOMS** | | |
| Toilet Brush | Either have one that locks into the container or keep the brush out of reach. | 5 min. |
| Poisons | Keep in secure, childproof cabinets or on high shelves. | 15–30 min. |
| Toilets | Keep the lids closed. Do *not* use automatic toilet-cleaning chemicals. | Constant (Start making it a habit!) |
| Cabinets | Keep secured with childproof locks. | 15–30 min. |
| **LAUNDRY ROOM** | | |
| Clothing | Store both clean and dirty clothes off the floor and out of reach. | 15–30 min. |
| Poisons (bleach, pods/detergent, dryer sheets, etc.) | Keep in secure, childproof cabinets or on high shelves. | 15 min. |

| Hazards | Fixes | Time Estimate |
|---|---|---|
| **AROUND THE HOME** | | |
| Plants | Keep off the floor. | 45 min.–1 hour |
| Trash Cans | Have a lockable trash can or keep it in a secure location. | 10–30 min. |
| Electrical Cords/ Window Blind Cords | Hide cords or make sure they are out of reach; pay particular attention to entertainment and computer areas. | 1–1.5 hours |
| Poisons | Check to make sure there aren't any poisons in reach (WD40, window/screen cleaner, carpet cleaner, air freshener); move all poisons to a central, locked location. | 1 hour |
| Windows | Be sure cords are out of reach in all rooms. | 1–2 hours |
| Fireplaces | Store cleaning supplies and tools where the dog can't get into them. Cover the fireplace opening with something the dog can't knock over. | 10 min. |
| Stairs | Cordon off so your puppy can't go up or down the stairs; make sure to test all puppy gates for safety. | 10–15 min. |
| Coffee Tables/ End Tables/ Nightstands | Clear off dangerous objects (e.g., scissors, sewing equipment, pens, and pencils) and all valuables. | 30–45 min. |

You should check for all these things periodically or at least annually.

If you have a cat, keep the litter box off the floor. It needs to be somewhere that your cat can easily get to, but your dog cannot access it. Since this involves training your cat, it's something you should do well in advance of the dog's arrival. You don't want your cat to undergo too many significant changes all at once. The new canine in the house will be enough of a disruption. If your cat associates the change with your new dog, you may find the feline refusing to use the litter box.

## Outdoor Hazards and Fixes

The area outside your home also needs dog-proofing. As with the inside, you will need to get down low and inspect all areas from a pup's perspective. If you get an adult dog, you will also need to do a check to ensure that your dog can't access things higher up. For example, keep poisons, such as fertilizer, car liquids, and chemicals, locked up or secured instead of leaving them on top of counters and shelves.

Remember to also post the vet's number in one of the sheltered outdoor areas in case of an emergency.

| Hazards | Fixes | Time Estimate |
|---|---|---|
| **GARAGE** | | |
| Poisons | Keep in secure, childproof cabinets or on high shelves (e.g., car chemicals, cleaning supplies, paint, lawn care)—this includes fertilizer. | 1 hour |
| Trash Bins | Keep them in a secure location. | 5 min. |
| Tools (e.g., lawn, car, hardware, power tools) | Make sure all cords are kept out of reach and never hang over the side of surfaces. | 30 min. –1 hour |
| Equipment (e.g., sports, fishing) | Keep out of reach, and never allow them to hang over the side of surfaces. | Constant (Start making it a habit!) |
| Sharp Implements | Keep out of reach, and never allow them to hang over the side of surfaces. | 30 min. |
| Bikes | Store off the ground or in a place your dog cannot reach (to keep the pup from biting the tires). | 20 min. |

| Hazards | Fixes | Time Estimate |
| --- | --- | --- |
| **FENCING (CAN BE DONE CONCURRENTLY)** | | |
| Breaks | Fix any breaks in the fencing. You need to make sure your dog can't easily get out of your yard. | 30 min.–1 hour |
| Gaps | Fill in any gaps so your dog doesn't escape. | 30 min.–1 hour |
| Holes/Dips at Base | Fill in any area that can be easily crawled under. | 1–2 hours |
| Yard | | |
| Poisons | Don't leave any poisons in the yard. | 1–2 hours |
| Plants | Verify that low plants aren't poisonous; fence off anything that is (such as grapevines). | 45 min.–1 hour |

Just like with the inside check, you will need to inspect the outside of your home quarterly or at least a couple of times a year. We tend to be less cautious with tools and chemicals outside because they are less obvious than they are inside the home.

## Creating a Safe, Escape-Proof Yard

Pool covers may not always be enough, so make sure to have fencing or some other kind of deterrent to keep your dog safe. Even if your dog loves swimming, make sure you're always around when he is in the pool. Dogs tend to be excellent swimmers, but that doesn't mean they know when they've hit their limits. Not all breeds are good swimmers, so ensuring your dog can't access your pool, spa, pond, or other large body of water is important.

Never leave your dog alone in the garage. He may be in the garage when you take car trips, which is why it's important to dog-proof this area.

Make room in your schedule for monthly inspections because dogs may dig out of boredom or damage a fence. Also, you should never leave your dog alone outside. Always attend to your dog when he goes out to the bathroom or to play because, when bored, most breeds will dig, explore, or do things that they shouldn't simply

because they know they aren't being watched. If your dog is a digger, there's a chance that any alone time outside will be the perfect time to turn soft dirt around your fence into a gaping hole for escape.

Some dogs break through or knock over fences because they want to hang out with the people on the other side of the fence. Even chain-link fences aren't entirely a deterrent because some dogs are both smart and athletic enough to be able to climb out.

You should create an area with shade and shelter for your dog for when you want to play outside during spring and summer days. Make sure to use pet-friendly materials for your dog's paws. Avoid things like sharp stones and harsher materials, as well as things that may be slippery. Avoid materials that retain heat so the dog is able to lie down and cool off from playing when it's warm.

# Protecting Elderly Dogs

Older dogs need some very specific environmental aspects addressed. Accommodations you should make for your senior dog include the following:

- Set water bowls out in a couple of different places so your canine can easily reach them as needed. If your dog shows signs of having trouble drinking or eating, place slightly raised water dishes around the home.

- Cover hard floor surfaces (such as tile, hardwood, and vinyl). Use nonslip carpets or rugs.

- Add cushions and soft bedding for your dog. There are bed warmers for dogs if your pet has achy joints or muscles. Of course, you also need to make sure he isn't too warm, so this can be a fine balancing act.

- Stay inside in extreme heat and cold. An old canine cannot handle extreme temperature changes as well as he once did.

- Use stairs or ramps for your dog wherever possible so the old pup doesn't have to try to jump. Do not pick up your older dog, as this can harm him. It may be slower, especially if your dog is losing sight, but helping your dog up steps and ramps is not only better for his activity levels, but when you praise him for it, this is uplifting for your dog.

- Avoid moving your furniture around, particularly if your canine shows signs of having trouble with his sight or has dementia. A familiar home is more comforting and less stressful as your pet ages. If your dog isn't able to see as clearly as he once did, keeping the home familiar will make it easier for him to move around without getting hurt.

- Consider setting up an area where your old dog can stay without having to go up and down any stairs too often.

- Create a space where your senior dog can relax with fewer distractions and noises. Don't make your old friend feel isolated, but do give him a place to get away from everyone if he needs to be alone.

None of these suggestions are particularly difficult or costly to implement, but they can make a world of difference to your canine companion.

# A Healthy and Nurturing Home

A holistic approach goes much farther than simply protecting your dog from potential dangers. Your home is set up to be comfortable for you, and it should be just as comfortable for your dog.

## Cleanliness

A clean home reduces things like mold and mildew, insects, and parasites that your dog may bring in (such as fleas and ticks). By keeping the floors clear, you reduce the risk of your dog getting hurt. When dogs get excited, they tend to be fairly reckless.

If there are things in the way when your pet hears the word "walkies" and dashes to the door, they could end up being a tripping hazard.

Use cleaners that are pet-friendly, not products that leave strong scents and traces of chemicals. There has been a trend over the last decade toward using nontoxic household cleaners. For example, you can make a pet-friendly spray that reduces the risk of insects (like ants and mites) by mixing the following:

- 1 cup of distilled vinegar
- 1 cup of water
- A couple drops of peppermint essential oil

Any area where your dog may place his paws should be sanitized with a dog-safe cleaner.

Since most breeds shed, make vacuuming a regular part of your daily schedule to keep the dust and dog hair accumulation to a minimum. Vacuums that have an allergen-capturing filter can help reduce both, which could also help with any allergies. Use attachments to clean:

- Dog beds

- Corners of the room and around furniture where dog hair is likely to accumulate

- Furniture (if your dog is allowed on it)

- The area around the food and water bowls (If you place a towel under the bowls, make sure to wash it regularly.)

You should also be cleaning your dog's food and water bowls daily. If you have stainless steel bowls, you won't need to use a special cleaner often (if at all) to get the bowls clean. The exception is if you give your dog raw meat, in which case you need to wash the bowl with a pet-safe dish soap and hot water after every meal.

Your dog's bed should be washed regularly. Follow the instructions that came with the bed. If it's safe to wash the dog bed cover, put it through the wash with things like dog towels, blankets, rugs, and toys. You can use baking soda if you want to remove some of that dog smell. A quick check of your detergent should help you identify if it's safe for pets. If the bedding cover can't be removed, make sure to regularly vacuum it. Rotate the towels and blankets you use for your dog—that will help them to last long.

## Air Quality

The following are some of the things you should do to improve the air quality in your home, both for you and your dog:

- Never smoke inside—secondhand smoke can cause cancer in your dog's nasal passages and lungs.

- Regularly change the air filters in your vents and AC unit because dust, dirt, dander, and pollen accumulate. If you live in a place with forest fires, ash can get in the filter.

- Use caution with fireplaces, especially with real logs.

Clean up your dog's waste in the yard regularly. Not only does this help keep you from walking through dog feces, but it will keep you and your dog from tracking it inside.

# Creating a Sleeping Area for Your Dog

Just like you have a bedroom, your dog should have a designated sleeping space that only belongs to him. Your dog's age will determine where you set up this space. For example, if you bring home a puppy, the space will need to be penned-in to keep the puppy from roaming free. If you have an older dog, the space needs to be somewhere that is easily accessible, doesn't have tripping hazards, and gives him a place to get away from activity as needed.

## Crates

Most dogs do well with a crate—it's kind of like a dog bedroom. Be sure the crate and bedding are set up before your dog arrives. A small, cozy space will help your dog feel comfortable while also dissuading him from using it as a restroom since he won't be able to get away from any mess he makes. If you feed your dog in the crate, he will start to associate it with positive things.

Never treat the crate like it's a prison for your puppy or adult dog. It's meant to be a safe haven after overstimulation or a comfortable place to go when it's time to sleep. Ensure your dog never associates the crate with punishment or negative emotions. You can get your puppy a carrying crate in the early days to make trips to the vet easier. Both puppies and adult dogs are going to spend a good bit of time in the crate in the early days, though adults will be able to roam around your home a lot faster.

For large breeds, you will probably need two crates if you bring a puppy home because puppies shouldn't have enormous open crates—and a large dog shouldn't have a crate that is barely big enough for him.

## Puppy Sleeping Space

When you bring home a puppy, you need to make sure to provide a safe space where he has access to you when he's scared at night. This means creating an area in your bedroom. The puppy's bed should be tucked into his crate, and the entire area should be blocked off to be sure no one can get in (and the puppy can't get out) during the night. This sleeping area should be close to where people are so the puppy doesn't feel abandoned. If you were able to get a blanket or pillow that smells like the dog's mother, make sure that it is in your puppy's space. Consider adding a little white noise (like an old-fashioned alarm clock) to cover unfamiliar sounds that could scare your new pet.

## Adult Dogs

You can set up a dog couch in your living room for when everyone is active around the home, but your dog needs a break. Some dogs still prefer a crate, which is perfect for things like thunderstorms and fireworks that could scare them.

At a minimum, your dog should have a comfortable bed and some blankets. Some dogs will carry a favorite toy around, and that may come with them when they go to bed. Usually, you don't want to have toys in the sleeping space as that invites play instead of encouraging rest.

## Choosing Chew Toys, Blanket, and Bedding

As they age, some dog breeds outgrow the desire to chew, but just as many don't. They will go after anything they can get their mouth on, especially if they suffer from separation anxiety or boredom.

That's why it's critical to get items that are safe for your dog.

## Materials

You should choose natural materials for dog toys. The following are types of materials that are safe for dogs:

- Wool
- Natural rubber (This applies to tennis balls as well.)
- BPA-free food grade silicon
- Eco-friendly cotton
- Hemp
- Jute

Most other materials should be avoided. If your dog is a chewing enthusiast and likes to annihilate toys, stuffed animals are not good because he's likely to eat the stuffing. If your dog is calmer and tends to just suck on stuffed animals, then they can be a source of comfort when he is home alone—especially if a stuffed toy smells like you. Probably the best item for chewers is an item of your clothing that you don't plan to wear anymore. This will give the dog something to cuddle while you are away.

You should also avoid toys that are hard because they can damage the dog's teeth.

Finally, avoid any toys that may grow larger if they get wet. Your dog is going to be carrying the toy around in his mouth, and that means it will start expanding. There's also a risk of the toy being dropped in water (whether a water bowl, puddle, or somewhere outside in the rain), so these types of toys are choking hazards. The best example of this is water beads, which can cause your dog significant health problems.

## Dog Size

If your dog can swallow a toy, then you need to get rid of it. Similarly, you don't want to get a toy that is too big for a small dog. You don't want your dog tripping or falling down the stairs because his vision is blocked.

Always be careful about toys with squeakers. These can be torn out and may get stuck in a dog's throat, so the best way to protect your dog is to only give him those toys when you are home. It can also be one more reason why your dog is so happy to see you.

## Old Toys

If you periodically clean your dog's toys with hot water and mild dish soap, they can last for a long time. That said, toys do get shredded over time, making them an ingestion hazard. If a toy is ripped, frayed, or has had the squeaker exposed, throw it away. Use this as a chance to get your canine companion something new and exciting.

## Potty Pads

If your pooch is already house-trained, you probably don't need pads in your home. However, if you have a puppy or an older dog with some bladder control issues, then you may need potty pads. If that's the case, these are the things you should consider when picking out the pads:

- Make sure your dog is comfortable with the pads. Don't buy too many of them until you know your dog will use them.

- Make sure the pads are easy to clean up. You're going to be changing them regularly, so you don't want it to be a more complicated and dirty task than it will already be.

- Make sure the pads are comfortable for potty training, especially for puppies. You don't want a puppy to be distracted. It may take a while to train older dogs just because they have more experience holding it in the house.

Eventually, you will want to wean your puppy off the pads. For older dogs, the pads are probably going to be a fact of life, even if you increase the number of times you take your dog outside. If that isn't possible, such as when you aren't home, you should have the pads in a place that is easily accessible for your elderly dog but far enough away from your dog's space that he won't be fouling his own area. You don't want your older dog to feel worse because his waste is located near where he eats or sleeps.

## Teaching Children about Proper Dog Care

You will need to be firm with children to make sure they don't accidentally hurt your dog or teach him to be too hyperactive. As he gets bigger, your puppy can become a potential danger if he is reckless around your children. This is more true for larger breeds, but small dogs can still be a problem as they can get up enough speed to knock children over.

To help your canine feel comfortable in his new home, you must make sure your children are careful and gentle with the dog, whether it's a puppy or an adult. Some kids may try to treat the puppy like a toy— don't let them. Take the time to make sure your children follow all the rules from the very beginning to ensure your puppy feels safe, happy, and isn't accidentally injured.

The following are the Five Golden Rules your children should follow from day one. They apply both to puppies and adult dogs, no matter the breed:

1. Always be gentle and respectful.
2. Do not disturb the puppy during mealtimes.
3. Chase is an outside game.
4. The puppy's four paws should always remain firmly on the ground. Never pick him up.
5. All valuables should be kept out of the puppy's reach.

Since your kids are going to ask why these rules are necessary, the following are some explanations you can use. If necessary, modify the discussion to meet the audience—what you say to a toddler is a lot different from what you should tell a teen about playing with your dog.

The vast majority of dog breeds tend to love children. You do still need to monitor younger children until you know your dog won't become too excited. Younger children may get a little too rough, and no matter how sturdy canines are, you don't want your new family member to get hurt by an overexcited child.

## Always Be Gentle and Respectful

At no time should anyone be rough with a puppy. It's important to be respectful of your puppy to help him learn to also be respectful toward people and other animals.

This rule must be applied consistently every time your children play with your puppy. Be firm if you see your children getting too excited or rough. You don't want the puppy to get overly excited either because he might end up nipping or biting someone. If he does, it won't be his fault because he is still learning. Make sure your children understand the possible repercussions if they get too rough.

## Mealtime

Dogs can be protective of their food, especially if you rescue a dog that has previously had to fend for himself. Even if you have a puppy, you don't want him to feel insecure during his mealtime because he will then learn to be aggressive whenever he eats. Save yourself, your family, and your dog future problems by making sure mealtime is his time alone. Teach your children their own mealtime is off-limits to the puppy as well.

No feeding your new dog from the table! From toddlers to teens, this is something you'll really need to emphasize—particularly for foods your kids don't like. Canines are pets, not garbage disposals, and no amount of cute puppy eyes should be rewarded with scraps from the table. That is a recipe for disaster, as it will get harder to convince your dog to stop begging if other people aren't following your rules. Some foods your dog shouldn't eat that could get slipped under the table. You can include some of the same food you make for the family for your dog, but that should be served on a plate.

## Chase

Make sure your children understand why a game of chase may be all right outdoors (though you'll need to monitor things), but inside the house, chasing is off-limits! A three-month-old puppy is hard enough to control when he is excited and running inside the house, but a 40-pound, eight-month-old puppy will be difficult to manage and can do a lot of damage. A 120-pound Great Dane puppy is going to be unmanageable and destructive.

Running inside your home gives your puppy the impression your home isn't safe for him because he's being chased; it also teaches your puppy that running indoors is allowed, which can be dangerous as the dog gets older and bigger. One of the last things you want to see is your adult dog barreling through your home—knocking into people and furniture—because he learned it was fine to run in the house when he was a puppy!

## Paws on the Ground

It doesn't matter how adorable your dog is—he is a living, breathing creature, and he needs to have his paws on the ground (even though he will quickly grow too big to pick up). You might want to carry your new family member around or play with the pup like a baby, but you and your family will have to resist that urge. The younger your children are, the more difficult it will be for them to understand the difference. It's so tempting to treat the puppy like a baby, but this is uncomfortable and unhealthy for him.

Older children will quickly learn that a puppy's nip or bite hurts a lot more than one would think. Those little teeth are quite sharp, and if a dog nips, he could accidentally be dropped—no one wants that to happen. If your children are never allowed to pick up the puppy, things will be a lot better for everyone involved. Remember, this also applies to you, so don't make things difficult by doing something you constantly tell your children not to do.

## Keep Valuables Out of Reach

Your kids will be less than happy if their personal possessions are chewed up by an inquisitive puppy, so teach them to put toys, clothes, and other valuables far out of reach. Depending on the size and intelligence of your dog, you may need to get creative. Cupboards, drawers, and other types of cabinets will probably be essential to ensure your dog can't access things you don't want to be destroyed. Some breeds will need these safety measures indefinitely because they may always need protection from themselves.

## Living in a Harmonious Home with Multiple Pets

Harmonious living is the goal, and that can be difficult, especially when you bring a new dog into the home. It can be a bit tricky introducing new dogs to a home with small animals and cats. Even puppies may want to chase those animals. To get the most well-rounded dog possible, you should start socializing him with your other dogs or pets when he's still a puppy. In most cases, this is a fairly straightforward process as long as your established pets are comfortable with you bringing a new dog into their home. Even cats may find they can put up with your new dog as long as you can convince your new dog not to chase them. Depending on your new dog's prey drive, this could prove to be a real challenge in the early days. Plan to have a space where your canine can't go so the cats have somewhere they feel safe.

The following are important tasks you should complete when preparing your current pets for the new arrival:

- Set up a schedule of activities and the people who will need to participate.

- Preserve your current dog's favorite places and furniture; make sure your current dog's toys and other personal items are not in the puppy's or new dog's space.

- Have playdates at your home to observe your dog's reaction to having an addition to the house.

Most dog breeds prefer a regular schedule, their own space, and playdates for a bit of extra fun.

## Stick to a Schedule

It's essential to have a schedule. Obviously, the new dog (especially if you bring home a puppy) is going to receive a lot of attention in the beginning, so you need to make a concerted effort to be sure your current pet(s) know you still care for them. Set a specific time in your schedule when you can show your current dog(s) how much you love him (them), and make sure you don't stray from that schedule after the puppy arrives.

When you bring the puppy home, plan to have at least one adult present for each dog you have in your home. If you have a cat in the home, the introduction will need to be slow and methodical. If you bring home an adult dog, you will need to be careful and keep the dog and cat separated when you aren't around to monitor them. Over time, it's likely the animals will learn to be fine with each other. If not, you will need to make sure that they're safely separated when you are gone.

Having a schedule in place for your other dogs will make it easier to follow the plan with the puppy. Once he has arrived, your puppy is going to eat, sleep, and spend most of the day and night in his assigned space. This means your puppy's space cannot block your current canine's favorite furniture, bed, or anywhere he rests during the day. None of your current dog's stuff should be in the puppy's area either; this includes toys. You don't want your older dog to feel as if the puppy is taking over his territory. Make sure your children also understand to never put your current dog's things in the puppy's area.

## Helping Your Current Dog Prepare for the Arrival of a New Dog

The following are strategies that will help prepare your current pooch for the arrival of your puppy or dog:

- Consider the personality of your dog to predict what might happen when the new family member arrives. If your current dog loves other dogs, this will probably hold true when the puppy shows up. If your current dog is territorial, you will need to be cautious when introducing the two dogs, at least until the new canine has become part of the pack. Excitable dogs need special attention to keep them from getting agitated when a new dog comes home. You don't want your current dog to be so excited that he makes the new dog feel threatened.

- Consider the times when unfamiliar dogs have been in your home. How did your current dog react to these other furry visitors? If your canine becomes territorial, be cautious when introducing your new pup. If you have never invited another dog into your home, organize a playdate with other dogs before your puppy arrives. You need to know how your current furry babies will react to new dogs in the house so that you can properly prepare. Meeting a dog at home is quite different from encountering one outside the home.

- Think about your established dog's interactions with other dogs for as long as you have known him. Has your dog shown protective or possessive behavior, either with you or others? Food is one of the reasons dogs will display aggression because they don't want anyone eating what is theirs. Some dogs can be protective of people and toys, too.

- If you know someone who owns a dog, organize a playdate so your current dog becomes aware of the temperament of other canines.

These same rules apply no matter how many dogs you have. Think about their individual personalities as well as how they interact together. Similar to humans, you may find when your dogs are together, they act differently. This is something you will need to keep in mind as you plan their first introduction.

There are always ways to improve the relationship between your pets, and it always starts with understanding how they interact with other animals and why. Sometimes, the problem could be jealousy. Make sure you're giving the same amount of time and energy to all of your pets.

# CHAPTER 5

# Healthy Habits to Adapt

There is a good reason why people compare having a dog to having a child—they require a lot of work. The big difference is dogs don't grow up. That's why it's important to establish healthy habits for your dog's care from the first day you bring him home.

Over the first few months, you'll learn how to work with your dog to get the best results. As with children, finding ways to make healthy habits fun will turn chores into great bonding time.

## Your Responsibilities

As a dog parent, you are fully responsible for your dog and his health. Some aspects of your dog will be genetically determined. For example, different breeds are prone to different ailments. It's up to you to ensure that your dog is healthy to the extent possible, even within any known health issues. For example, a dog breed may be prone to gaining weight; this is common for about half of breeds, with some breeds being considered nearly bottomless pits. The food you give your dog, as well as the amount and intensity of the exercise he gets, will ensure your pup doesn't reach an unhealthy weight for his size.

There are a number of regular tasks you will need to do to ensure the health of your dog beyond diet and exercise. These include:

- ☑ Regular physical exams, which will require more care after being in certain types of environments
- ☑ Home check-ups
- ☑ Bathing
- ☑ Brushing his coat and massaging
- ☑ Brushing his teeth
- ☑ Clipping toenails
- ☑ Training

All these tasks should become a regular part of your schedule. Sure, there may be times when you can skip a task. For example, your dog will likely need to be bathed more often during periods of the year when you are outside often. If you don't go out much, such as in the winter, you likely won't need to bathe your dog as often.

Dogs aren't able to tell you when they aren't feeling well or when something changes. It's your responsibility to keep an eye out for issues. For example, brushing your dog is the perfect time to make sure he has a healthy coat.

# How to Examine Your Dog

Research has found that petting your dog has a calming effect on you. While your dog is helping you reduce stress, you can use that chance to return the favor by doing an examination to make sure your best friend doesn't have any early signs of a health issue.

The following is a checklist to help you establish regular healthy habits for your dog:

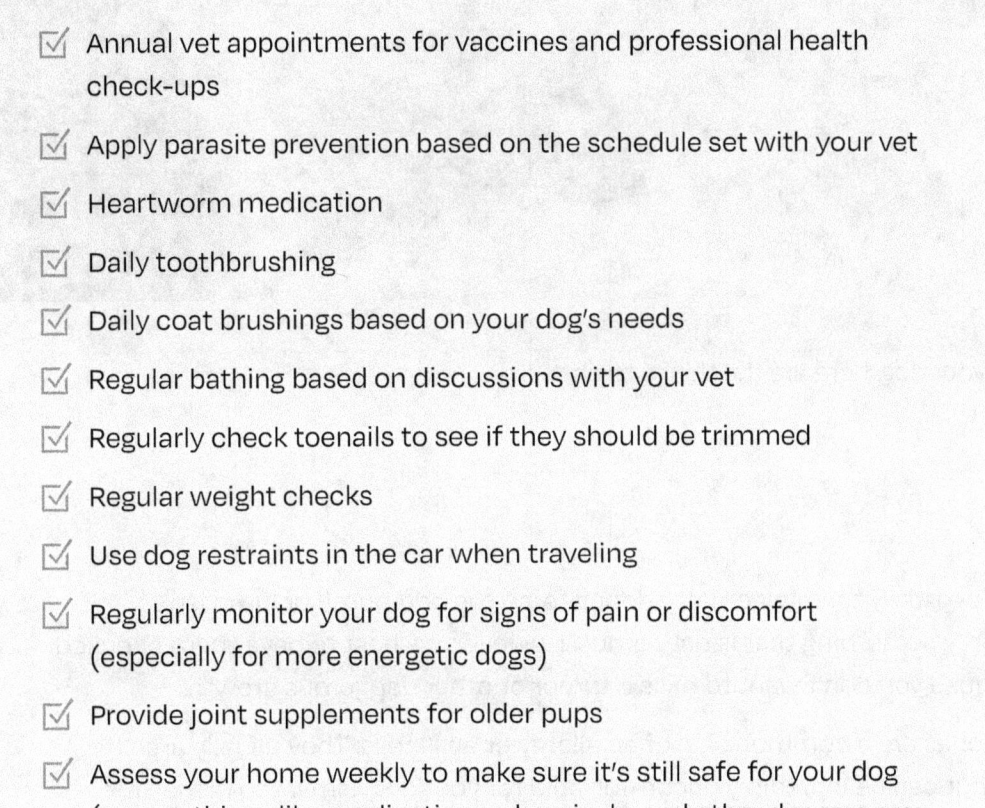

- ☑ Annual vet appointments for vaccines and professional health check-ups
- ☑ Apply parasite prevention based on the schedule set with your vet
- ☑ Heartworm medication
- ☑ Daily toothbrushing
- ☑ Daily coat brushings based on your dog's needs
- ☑ Regular bathing based on discussions with your vet
- ☑ Regularly check toenails to see if they should be trimmed
- ☑ Regular weight checks
- ☑ Use dog restraints in the car when traveling
- ☑ Regularly monitor your dog for signs of pain or discomfort (especially for more energetic dogs)
- ☑ Provide joint supplements for older pups
- ☑ Assess your home weekly to make sure it's still safe for your dog (ensure things like medications, chemicals, and other dangers are not in easy reach of your dog, both inside and outside)

Some of these items will need to be done often, while others may be required less frequently. Something like bathing will be dependent on your dog's breed and how dirty your pup gets. Your vet should be able to help you determine the best time frame for bathing your dog based on breed and coat length. Some dogs have natural oils that help their coats stay healthy, and over-bathing them can damage those natural oils.

When grooming your dog, here are the things to check:

## Skin and fur

- ☑ As dogs age, they tend to get fatty deposits, so the odd bump or lump isn't necessarily something that is dangerous. However, it's best to have them checked out because you don't want to miss a tumor or other dangerous growth.

- ☑ Bald patches are a common sign of an allergy or an illness. They usually aren't serious but can be incredibly uncomfortable for your dog, similar to rashes for humans. They should still be checked by a vet. Once an allergy is identified, it will be easier to help prevent your dog from having problems.

- ☑ Skin color changes could be a sign of a number of issues.

- ☑ Scaly-looking skin may indicate a yeast infection, common for older dogs. Yeast infections can cause balding and are often accompanied by a bad odor.

- ☑ When you brush your dog, make it a habit to check for fleas. Later in this book, we provide details on fleas and what to look for when grooming your dog. If you go hiking, take your dogs into the woods, or spend time in tall grass, do a thorough check for ticks after each hike. Ticks can carry illnesses like Lyme disease. If you find a tick, make an appointment as early as possible with the vet to have your dog checked.

# Head

☑ Regularly check your dog's eyes when you are grooming or bathing him. Some breeds are inclined to infection. Dogs that play outside a lot may scratch their eyes on branches, sticks, and other objects, so it is best to monitor them for issues. The following are signs of a potential eye problem:

- ☐ Redness
- ☐ Pus and other discharge
- ☐ Bad odor
- ☐ Excessive tears
- ☐ Scratching the eye
- ☐ Bumping into things often

☑ Monitoring your dog's ears for signs of a problem is important because the ears can trap dirt and encourage bacterial growth. When you brush your dog, give each ear a quick check for signs of inflammation and infection. Here's what to look for during these checks:

- ☐ Redness
- ☐ Bad odor
- ☐ Discharge
- ☐ Swelling
- ☐ Shaking of the head
- ☐ Scratching the ears

☑ Check your dog's nose daily for:

- ☐ Cracking
- ☐ Discharge
- ☐ Growths
- ☐ Sores
- ☐ Obstructions

☑ When you brush your dog's teeth, whether weekly or daily, look for the following potential issues:

- ☐ Plaque buildup
- ☐ Bad breath
- ☐ Blood on the gums
- ☐ Change in gum pigmentation
- ☐ Damage to the teeth

## Legs and Paws

☑ Lumps and bumps may form on your dog's legs or paws, which should be checked.

☑ Check your dog's nails to make sure they aren't too long. This will usually be something you can hear as long nails will click on tile, vinyl, hardwood, concrete, asphalt, etc.

☑ Check between your dog's toes to make sure dirt doesn't build up and objects don't get stuck in them. Also check the pads to make sure they aren't cracked and don't have things stuck in them. You should wash your dog's paws, including between the toes, during baths.

## Rump

☑ As gross as it may seem, you need to routinely check your dog's backside to make sure that there aren't any issues. Some breeds have issues that need regular care, particularly with their anal glands. An impacted anal gland creates a smell like rotting fish and will require care until you learn how to manage the issue. If your dog has a problem with his anal glands, take him to the vet. A professional needs to take care of it in the beginning. If it's a recurring problem, the vet may show you how to express the gland to remove the excess fluid. When selecting your dog, you can find out if the breed (or one of the breeds if getting a mixed dog) are prone to anal gland problems.

☑ Especially if your dog has a lot of fur around the rectal area or long fur under his tail, you will need to regularly clean and cut the fur so it doesn't get covered in waste.

There is a lot to look for, but once you're in the habit of checking your dog, it will become more obvious when there is something wrong.

It's important to note that these exams should be done in addition to regular vet check-ups.

## Deeper Home Check-Up Possibilities

If your dog is acting strange, such as being lethargic, losing his appetite, coughing, etc., you need to set up an appointment with your vet.

The following tips will help you determine if there are potential issues with your dog. For example, if you check your dog's temperature and find that it's normal but he has an elevated pulse, that can help identify an issue. It's also good information to take to your vet.

### Taking Your Dog's Temperature

An elevated temperature in dogs doesn't necessarily mean the animal is sick. It's possible that a pup just finished a vigorous activity, for example. However, if you notice your dog acting differently, you can check his temperature to see if it's possible he's coming down with an illness.

The following are signs that your dog may be running a fever:

- Acting lethargic
- Losing his appetite
- Sneezing constantly
- Has a glassy look in his eyes
- Panting
- Has a runny nose
- Shivering with no obvious cause (it's not cold, and there is no obvious stress to make the dog nervous)
- Vomiting
- Has a warm nose, ears, or both

Dogs tend to run a bit hotter than humans, usually having a temperature between 100°F and 102.5°F (38°C and 39.2°C).

- A temperature between 102.5°F and 104°F (39.2°C and 40°C) indicates a mild fever.

- A temperature over 104°F (40°C) is considered a high fever, and you should get your dog to the vet as quickly as possible.

There are forehead thermometers you can use to take your dog's temperature. Note that they're not entirely reliable because even if your dog is willing to sit still, his fur may make the reading less reliable.

Vets use rectal thermometers to take reliable temperatures. However, you need to have someone train you to use one, as there is a risk associated with taking a dog's temperature this way. The most obvious problem is that your dog isn't going to want to sit still for this procedure. You can hurt your pup by doing it wrong, so until you've actually had temperature-taking lessons from a vet, it's best to use less reliable forehead thermometers—they will at least give you an idea of whether your dog is running a fever.

If you don't want to use a thermometer, you can also

- Feel your dog's paws and ears. This is similar to checking his forehead because these areas tend to indicate a fever, and there is less fur in the way to dampen the heat.

- Feel your dog's nose. It may be hot, or there may also be a green or yellow discharge.

- Touch your dog's gums if he'll allow it. If they feel dry and warm and look a bit red, that's usually an indicator of a fever.

## Checking Your Dog's Heart Rate

To do this, you have to know what your dog's normal heart rate is. This is going to vary based on the size and breed of your dog. A Chihuahua has a faster resting heart rate than a Great Dane, for example. The slowest heart rate considered normal for dogs is 60 beats a minute. The fastest rate is more than twice that at 140 beats a minute, or over two beats a second. Get a baseline reading on your dog's heart rate when you're both at home relaxing.

Your dog's heart rate is going to change during different life stages as well. Set aside a day every year to check your dog's heart rate, then record it somewhere easy to find. Keep that baseline information handy to refer back to as needed.

Whether you are getting a baseline heart rate or checking your dog because you think he may be sick, the steps are the same.

1. Put your hand over the left side of your dog's chest.
2. Set a 15-second timer.
3. Count how many times your dog's heart beats in those 15 seconds.
4. Multiply the number of beats by four.

Most of the time, it's not a problem if your dog's heart skips a beat. Things like breathing can affect how quick the heart rate is. There is a common condition in dogs called respiratory sinus arrhythmia, where the heart skips a beat, and it isn't a cause for concern on its own.

A skipped beat is more of a concern if you notice other symptoms, such as your dog acting tired or losing his appetite.

If your dog's heart is going noticeably faster or slower than normal and there is no obvious cause, it's best to set up an appointment with your vet. This kind of problem is almost always accompanied by other symptoms—which is usually why people stop to check their dog's heart rate.

## Monitoring Your Dog's Breathing

Like his heart rate, your dog's breathing rate will vary based on size and breed. The range is 12 to 24 breaths a minute, so you should get a baseline for your dog so you can better monitor your dog's health. The steps to do this are simple.

- Place a hand on your dog's rib (either side is fine).
- Set a 15-second timer.
- Count how many times your dog's chest expands.
- Multiply the number of beats by four.

Pay attention to if your dog is making strange noises when breathing. This will be trickier to notice for some breeds, particularly brachial dogs, who tend to be noisy breathers. Breeds like Bulldogs and Pugs are going to make snorting noises and other sounds that you are probably already familiar with hearing. You should listen for sounds that are not normal for your dog.

Usually there will be other symptoms that will inspire you to check your dog's breathing. Knowing the baseline respiratory rate will help you to better determine when your dog's breathing is more rapid or slower than expected.

## Checking Your Dog's Hydration

Making sure that your dog remains hydrated is an important part of taking care of him. It's important for you to be constantly aware of your dog's water bowl, as some breeds go through a lot of water. All dogs tend to drink a lot after vigorous exercise. Your dog will almost certainly drink when needed as long as you keep water in the bowl.

When your dog gets sick, though, it's possible that he could get dehydrated. If this happens, you need to get your dog to the vet ASAP. The following are signs of dehydration in dogs:

- Appetite loss
- Dry nose and gums
- Eyes look sunken
- Less energy
- Lethargic
- Panting
- Saliva is thicker
- Skin is less elastic

If you aren't sure, you can do a skin test to check to see if your dog is suffering from dehydration.

1. Gently pinch the skin near your dog's shoulders.
2. Raise the skin up and release it.
3. Watch to see how the skin reacts:
   a. If it snaps back into place quickly, your dog is staying hydrated.
   b. If it does not immediately snap back into place, then your dog is probably not getting enough to drink or is dehydrated because of an ailment.

Like the other tests, you should get a baseline of how quickly your dog's skin snaps back into place when you know he is healthy. This will help you to see when it doesn't happen as quickly as it should.

Always get your dog to the vet as quickly as possible if you believe he's dehydrated. In the meantime, there are a few things you can do to help your dog.

- Get your dog some cool, fresh water.

- Give him ice, especially chips. Some dogs can be excited by this, so it could be a game to get your dog to have some extra water during hot days of the year by tossing him ice chips.

- Give your dog a fluid with electrolytes, including things like Pedialyte. Don't do this if your dog has been vomiting. Consult a vet for how much to give your dog.

If your dog has been vomiting for more than a day or has been having diarrhea for a day or two, make sure to check that he is staying hydrated. The more dehydrated a dog is, the less he'll eat, and that can exacerbate the problem, as food has some natural liquid that can help your dog stay hydrated.

## Bathing

In most cases, it's best to bathe your dog at home. It's great bonding time, and your dog is more likely to be relaxed with you than with a stranger. However, there are some breeds where having a professional groomer is going to be a better idea— some coats just need special care.

If you decide to use a groomer for bathing, make sure that you know what products they use. You want to ensure they are using natural and dog-nose-friendly products that will be better for your best friend.

When bathing your dog yourself, first, make sure the water isn't too cold or too hot but comfortably warm, and always avoid getting your dog's head wet.

1. Gather everything you will need before you start your dog's bath. At a minimum, you need the following:

   a. Shampoo and conditioners made specifically for dogs
   b. Cup for pouring water (if bathing in a tub)
   c. Towels
   d. Brushes for after the drying process
   e. Nonslip tub mat if you use a tub
   f. Buckets and a hose to rinse off if you bathe your dog outside

2. Take your dog out for a walk. This will tire him and make him a little hotter and less fearful—he might even appreciate the bath's cooling effect.

3. Run the water, making sure the temperature is lukewarm and not hot, especially if you have just finished a walk. If you are washing your dog in a bathtub, you only need enough water to cover your puppy's stomach. Do not fully cover your dog's body.

4. Pick up your dog if you are using a bathtub, and talk in a strong, confident voice.

5. Place the dog in the tub and use the cup to wash him. Don't use too much soap—it isn't necessary. You can fully soak the dog, starting at the neck and going to the rump. It's fine to get him wet and suds him up all at once, or you can do it a little at a time if your dog is very wiggly. Just make sure you don't get any water on his head.

6. Confidently talk to your dog while you're bathing him.

7. Make sure you don't pour water on your dog's head or in his eyes or ears. Use a wet hand and gently scrub. (Follow the steps a little later in this section for how to wash his face and ears carefully.)

8. When you rinse your dog, make sure to brush up against the fur so that there is no shampoo left.

9. Take your dog out of the water and towel him dry.

10. Pay special attention to drying around the head and face.

11. Brush your dog when you're finished.

12. Give him a treat if he was particularly upset about the bath.

You can use these practices with other kinds of bathing, such as outside or at a public washing facility, modifying them as necessary.

The first few times you bathe your dog, pay attention to the things that bother him. If he's afraid of running water, make sure you don't have the water running when your dog is in the tub. If he moves around a lot when you start to apply the shampoo, it could indicate the smell is too strong. Modify the process as necessary in order to make it as comfortable for your dog as possible.

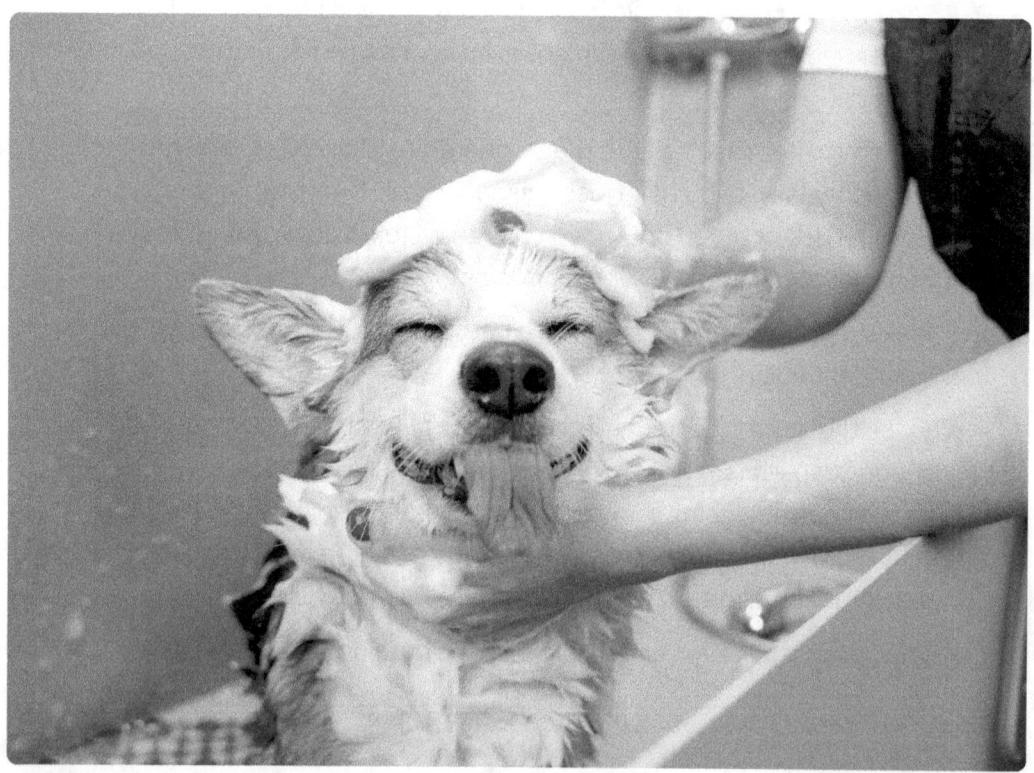

Keep a calm, loving tone as you wash your dog to make the process a little easier. Sure, he may whine, throw a tantrum, or wiggle excessively, but a calm reaction will teach your dog that bathing is a necessary part of being a member of the pack.

Most dogs will do better if you find a natural shampoo and other supplies. They don't have the kinds of chemicals and other additives that can irritate their skin and noses.

## Grooming

Most dogs will be a bit better for having daily brushings. This may get a bit tedious, and for short-haired breeds, it probably isn't necessary. However, it's something that most dogs enjoy, and it gives you some dedicated time with him every day. This means you will be more familiar with the moles, bumps, bruises, and other things on your dog's body so that you are more likely to notice when there is something wrong. The added bonus of regular brushing is that it improves your dog's circulation, which is beneficial, especially for older pooches.

Given how often dogs need to be groomed, it probably comes as a relief that you can easily take care of most of their needs at home. There are still a few things about caring for your dog (all paw-related) that we strongly recommend seeing an expert about in the early days. But for the most part, you should be able to take care of your dog's grooming needs yourself.

Dogs have an overcoat and an undercoat, both of which can mat and retain debris. You have two primary purposes for doing these regular brushings:

- Keep large mats from forming. This includes brushing around your dog's head and behind the ears, around the legs and tail, and along the chest—these are the areas where mats tend to form. If a large mat does form, it is better to trim the mat than to try to brush it out. Small mats and tangles can be removed with mat combs and slicker brushes.

- Remove the extra hair from the undercoat; this task can be significantly sped up if you have a high-velocity dryer or other quick method of removing the excess hair. You can also brush the undercoat by hand, but it will take a lot longer than using a tool designed to remove the fur. Either way, it can get messy because there will seem to be an endless supply of hair that needs to be removed.

Here's a quick summary of the best tools to properly groom your dog:

- Grooming comb for removing mats
- Slicker brush to gently spread your dog's natural oils over his body
- Small scissors to remove mats
- High-velocity dryer or undercoat rake
- Stripping knives, which are made based on a person's dominant hand, help remove extra undercoat fur
- Shampoo (make sure you use dog shampoo, not human, and check Bark Space for the latest recommendations)
- Nail trimmers
- Toothbrush and dog toothpaste

## Coat Management

Always make sure to tire your dog before you start brushing. You can't rush the process. To get all the tangles and other issues taken care of, you'll need your dog to sit still for a while. You'll know when you don't need to dedicate time to tiring your dog when he starts to slow down as a senior or shows an interest in just sitting and letting you pet and brush him.

For all ages, if mats are severe, it's much more humane to simply cut a mat than to drag out the removal process.

You will want to start with a coarse brush and remove tangles carefully as you go. After the tangles and small mats are removed, change to a slicker brush to spread the skin's natural oils through the coat.

### PUPPIES

The difficulty when grooming a puppy is fairly universal because puppies are notorious for squirming! Trying to tell your puppy that the brush is not a toy clearly won't work, so be patient during each brushing session!

Your pup will be so adorable that you probably won't mind a grooming session taking a bit longer than expected. Just make sure you let him know grooming is serious business, and playing comes after. Otherwise, your dog is going to always try to play, which will make brushing him even more time-consuming.

Try planning to brush your puppy after a vigorous exercise session. If you find your puppy has trouble sitting still, you can make brushing sessions shorter but do it more than once a day until he gets used to the routine.

## ADULT DOGS

Brushing needs to be done several times a week for adult dogs, especially after a lot of outdoor activity. Remember to start with the coarse brush to remove the tangles and smooth the hair, and then move to the slicker brush. The grooming process stimulates the skin to release oils that make the fur shinier and more resistant to dirt. If you regularly brush your dog, it can help reduce how often you have to bathe him.

If you rescued an adult dog, it might take a little while to get him used to being brushed frequently. If your dog doesn't feel comfortable in the beginning when you brush his fur, work the routine into your schedule, just like training, so he will get accustomed to the task.

## SENIOR DOGS

You can brush your senior dog more often if you would like, as the extra affection and time you give him will likely be welcome. You will probably find there are fewer tangles and small mats as your dog slows down, but the grooming process can be incredibly welcome in older dogs. Just relaxing with you will be enjoyable for him (and the warmth of your hands will feel really good on his aging body).

## Trimming Nails

If you have never cut a dog's nails before, do not start by practicing on your dog. Schedule an appointment with a professional groomer who has worked with large dogs with a lot of fur. There is a lot more work to do than just trimming the nails, and no novice should ever attempt this grooming activity without a lot of guidance. A professional can show you what needs to be done to trim the fur and then how to trim the nails. It is far harder to do with large dogs than with small dogs, and it's almost impossible with a dog that has a lot of fur around the nails or dark nails that are thicker and harder to trim.

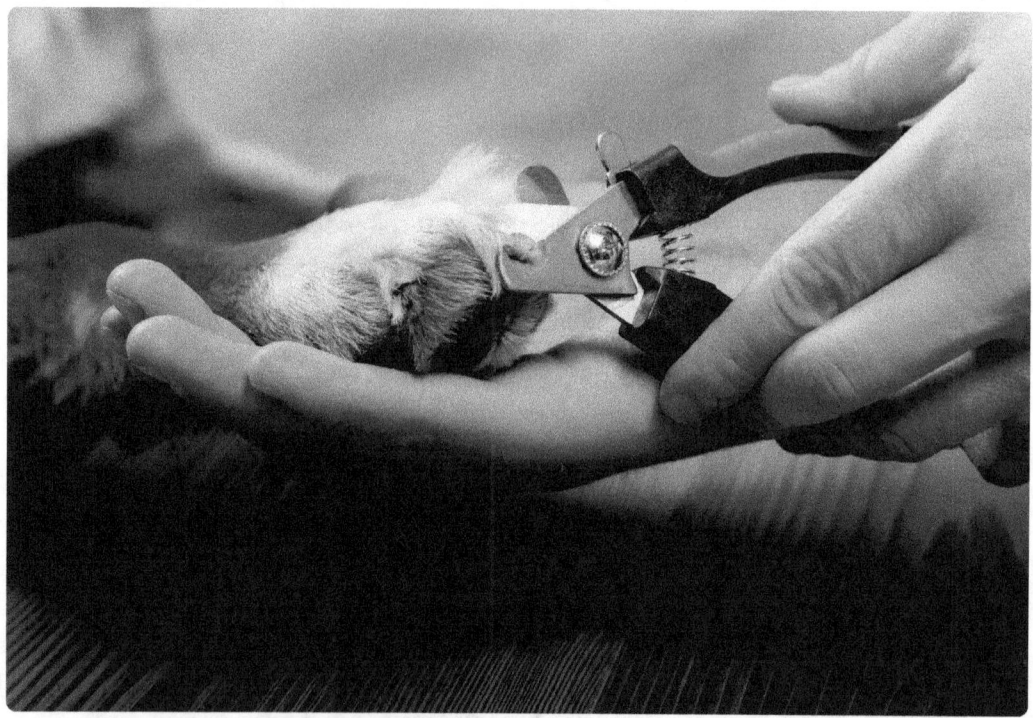

Even if you have experience with trimming a dog's nails, it's best to seek help from a professional, as the hair around the paws will need to be trimmed and managed before the cutting can begin.

Your professional can let you know how often your dog needs his nails trimmed based on how quickly he wears down his nails. If you and your dog spend a lot of time walking on sidewalks and concrete, nail growth will be slower than if you just take regular jaunts in woods and dirt paths.

## Cleaning Eyes and Ears

When bathing your dog, use a washcloth to wash his face and ears, and always avoid getting water in his ears, which can lead to problems.

You will need to make weekly checks around your dog's eyes and ears to detect infections early. The following are signs of a problem:

- Frequent head shaking or tilting
- Regular scratching at ears
- Swollen or red ears
- A smell or discharge from the ears

If you notice any problems with your dog's ears, make an appointment with your vet. Never try to treat an infection on your own; hydrogen peroxide, cotton swabs, and other cleaning tools should never be used in a dog's ears. Your vet can show you how to clean your dog's ears correctly.

Take the time to check your dog's eyes as you groom him. Cataracts are a fairly common problem for all dogs as they age.

## Oral Health

Dogs aren't prone to dental issues, but that doesn't mean you should skip brushing your dog's teeth. Besides healthy food, there are two recommendations for taking care of your dog's teeth.

- Brush your dog's teeth at least once a week.
- Give your dog dental chew treats.

### BRUSHING YOUR DOG'S TEETH

You have to learn to be patient and keep teeth cleaning from being an all-out fight with your dog. Brushing a dog's teeth is a little weird, and your pup may not be terribly happy with someone putting stuff in his mouth. However, once he is accustomed to it, the task will likely only take a few minutes a day. Regular brushing removes plaque and tartar, making your puppy's teeth healthier.

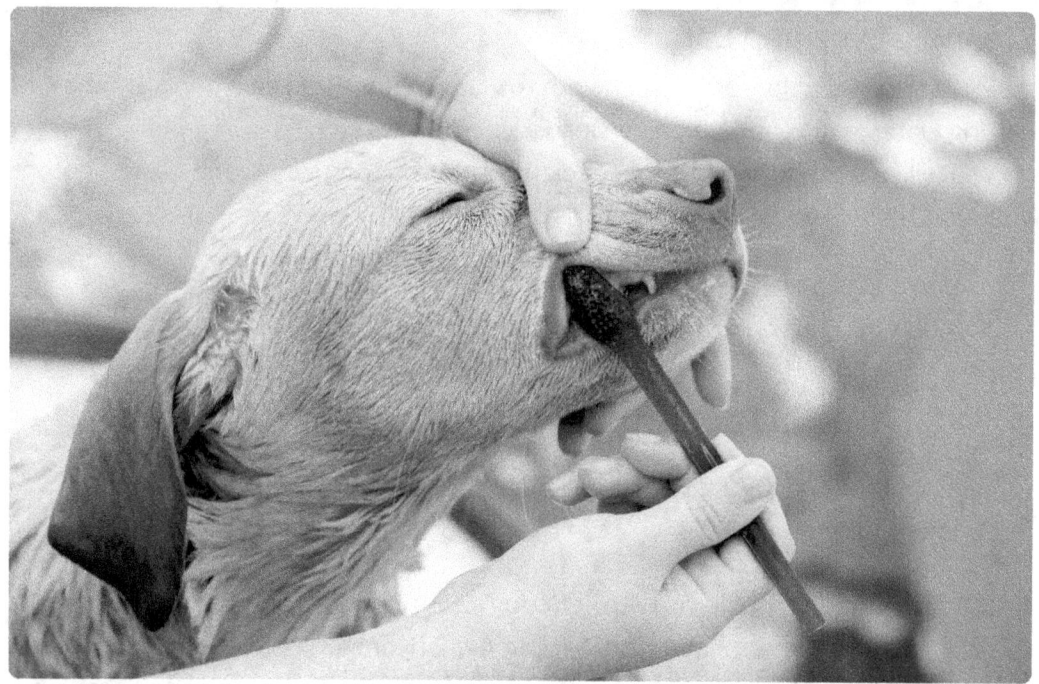

Always use a toothpaste made for dogs; human toothpaste can be toxic for your friend. There are assorted flavors of dog toothpaste, which will make it easier to brush your dog's teeth, and it could also be entertaining as he tries to eat the meat-flavored toothpaste!

The following are the steps for brushing your dog's teeth:

1. Put a little toothpaste on your finger and hold it out to your dog.
2. Let your dog lick the toothpaste from your finger.
3. Praise your dog for trying something new.
4. Put a little toothpaste on your finger again, lift your dog's upper lip, and begin to rub in circles along your dog's gums. Your pup will likely make it difficult by constantly trying to lick your finger. Give your puppy praise when he doesn't lick the toothpaste or doesn't wiggle too much.

   a. Try to move your finger in a circular motion. This will be very tricky, especially if you have a puppy with sharp baby teeth.

   b. Try to keep the dog still without putting him in a vise. As your puppy gets bigger, he'll need to know how to sit voluntarily for the cleaning process.

5. Try to massage both the top and bottom gums. It's likely the first few times you won't be able to do much more than get your finger in your dog's mouth, and that's okay. Over time, your dog will learn to listen because general behavioral training will reinforce listening to your commands.

6. Stay positive. No, you probably won't be able to clean your dog's teeth properly for a while, and that is perfectly fine—as long as you keep working at it patiently and consistently.

Once your dog seems comfortable having his teeth brushed with your finger, try the same steps with a canine toothbrush. (It could take a couple of weeks before you can graduate to this stage.)

## DENTAL CHEWS

One of the healthiest treats to give any dog is dental chews. They aren't a replacement for regular brushing, but they are a good complement. Dogs tend to love these treats, and they help improve your dog's breath, so it is a win-win. Make sure to do your research to ensure that you're giving your dog the healthiest dental chews. You don't want to give your dog any treats that have questionable or uncertain ingredients.

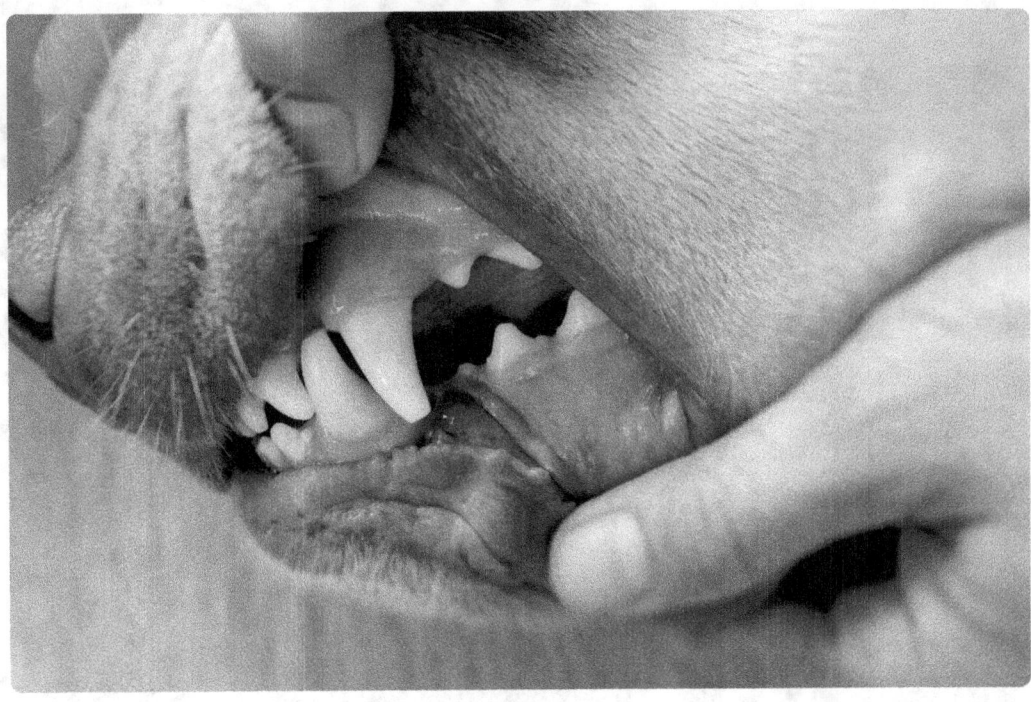

Section 3

# TRAINING AND ACTIVITIES

# CHAPTER 6

# Physical Activity and Socialization

Being physically and mentally active is important for all dog breeds. Even mellower dogs need to get adequate exercise to be healthy.

Another vital part of your dog's health is socialization. Making sure your dog has adequate socialization can ensure that he remains healthy and happy. If a dog isn't properly socialized, he will get scared of the outdoors, which can cause him to lash out.

Let's look at the best ways to keep your dog active and social for the best possible life.

## What Healthy Behavior Means for Your Dog—and for You

You need to be trained in how to train. If you don't have that kind of experience, the best way to create a healthy home for you, your family, and your dog is to enroll in training classes for both you and your dog.

From regular walks to getting out and being adventurous, you have to tailor your exercise routine to your dog's energy levels and abilities. If you and your family aren't active people, you should not be getting working dog breeds, such as Huskies, Dalmatians, and Weimaraners. These breeds are perfect for people who want jogging companions and hiking buddies. For people who prefer a more tempered exercise schedule, small-dog breeds, like Bulldogs, are the way to go.

When you get a dog with similar exercise needs as you, training him is so much easier, and it will help you to develop a healthier lifestyle that is perfect for your dog. Even better, it helps to create strong bonds with your dog.

## Proper Exercise and Training—Being a Responsible Dog Parent

As your dog's trainer, you are responsible for ensuring he gets the right amount of exercise every day. Since all dogs need to have at least basic training to behave, this can be a part of their mental activity, and you can use it when you are physically active. For example, if you are out for a walk with your dog and a fire truck goes by, telling your dog to sit can ensure that he doesn't try to chase the truck. However, physical exercise needs to focus on getting your dog enough movement throughout the day to be healthy.

You need to research breeds so that you know what the recommended exercise time is for your dog. If you have a dog with high exercise needs (some require between two and four hours a day), it's fine to break that up over the course of the day, with one vigorous 45-minute to hour-long exercise session, then several walks and training sessions to round out the rest of the time. On weekends and vacation days, you can spend a lot more time outdoors having fun.

If your dog isn't getting enough activity, it will probably be very obvious. He will take out his energy and boredom on your furniture, doors, and home because high-energy dogs have to be active—their bad behavior is your fault if you are not ensuring they are active enough. It can get dangerous if you don't meet a dog's exercise needs because being overweight will increase the potential for a lot of ailments, especially as your dog ages.

If you have a puppy, frequent 10-to-15-minute training sessions can be a good activity as well. Short walks can double as training sessions. You can try "Sit" and "Heel" during walks once your dog reaches a stage where he can do these commands well in your home.

You will have limits about how much cold and rainy weather you can handle. This doesn't mean that your canine can skip being active. Fortunately, there are plenty of indoor activities that you can do on days when going outside isn't such a good idea, as discussed later in this book.

## Bonding Through Activity

Exercise and activities are how people and dogs have bonded for thousands of years. In the early days, dogs and people hunted together. Over time, they learned to do other things as well. Today, people take dogs hiking, swimming, jogging, and do a wide range of other leisure activities with them. While you are looking out for your dog's health, he's also looking after yours by encouraging you to exercise regularly.

## The Importance of Physical Activity

The purpose of physical activity is the same for dogs as for humans—they were made to be active, not to sit around all day. Exercise helps them to maintain (or meet) a healthy weight, improves their immune systems, builds muscles, and helps their circulation. Most importantly, it makes them happy. Being active is necessary for most dogs to feel a sense of satisfaction.

All dogs require some physical activity; the only question is how much is right for your dog. It's important to remember that your vet will need to clear young dogs (especially if they are still puppies) before you start doing activities that include sustained running or jogging. The dog's bones and joints need to finish growing before you put that kind of strain on them. Since you will need to do a good bit of training in the early days, you should have more than enough activities to keep your dog happily entertained so that he gets physically and mentally tired without jogging. It's much easier to tire a five-month-old high-energy puppy than a five-year-old high-energy dog.

There are nearly as many activities available to dogs as there are for people—swimming, hiking, long walks, exploring trails, or sniffing along the beach. When your active day is over, dogs make fantastic cuddle buddies as you relax.

## Exercise for Your Dog

It's important to remember that exercise isn't just about getting a dog physically tired. When you exercise, your goal isn't to be so exhausted at the end that you need a nap. Exercise meets the following needs:

- It fosters muscle development in young dogs and people.
- It helps maintain muscle tone in adults.
- It encourages better metabolism.
- It stimulates the brain and body.
- It helps to improve focus—and in dogs that translates to better behavior.
- It boosts the immune system.

## Understanding Your Dog's Exercise Needs

You need to do some research as you calculate the exercise needs for your dog.

- **Breed** — this is the factor that will require the most research, especially if you have a mixed-breed dog. Breeds that are accustomed to hard work have a lot more energy, so they require a lot more daily exercise.

- **Size** — larger breeds always need more exercise. A small dog gets a lot more exercise during a 30-minute walk because his legs have to move two or three times faster to keep up with you. Large dogs need more exercise both because their strides are so much bigger and because they tend to have joint issues. Keeping their muscles strong is important to keep their joints as healthy as possible.

- **Age** — the type of exercise that works best for your dog depends in large part on his age. Puppies have a lot of energy, but things like obedience training and basic training also count toward their exercise needs ... and they tire so much faster. Older dogs don't need as much exercise and often aren't able to exercise like they did as adults.

- **Health** — dogs that have health issues don't require as much exercise and often aren't capable of vigorous exercise. You have to tailor their exercise schedule to meet their abilities and health. Sometimes the health issues are temporary, such as a bad reaction to a shot or a communicable illness. Other ailments may require permanent changes to how you and your dog exercise.

- **Body type** — your dog's body will help to dictate a lot about the way he should exercise and for how long. Greyhounds are a large breed, but their exercise needs are much less than the equally large Labrador Retriever. The most important consideration, though, is the dog's face. Brachial dogs, or dogs that have a flat snout, such as Pugs and Bulldogs, don't need as much exercise. More importantly, they can't safely participate in vigorous activities because their flat noses cause them problems with breathing. They get hotter much faster since they aren't able to pant as efficiently as dogs with longer noses.

All of these are factors you need to consider as you move into the next section—your exercise schedule. Take the time to research your dog's breed to get a baseline for what is needed.

## Creating Your Dog's Exercise Schedule

One thing dogs have in common with humans is that if they aren't made to exercise, they won't. You can't simply send your dog into your yard and expect him to exercise. Most dogs will chase animals that are in the yard, but that's often the most exercise they will get—and that isn't nearly enough.

You need an exercise schedule both for your dog and for you.

Most breeds love a schedule, but you should also mix up what you do to keep your dog engaged in the activity. Taking the same walk every day is not going to be mentally engaging, and your dog will likely get bored.

Create a schedule using your phone or a hard-copy calendar in your home. Given how difficult it can be to do something different on the weekdays, you can add something like the following:

| | |
|---|---|
| MONDAY | 1-hour walk at the park |
| TUESDAY | 30-minute morning walk around the neighborhood; 30-minute evening walk around the neighborhood |
| WEDNESDAY | 1-hour walk at the park |
| THURSDAY | 30-minute morning walk around the neighborhood; 30-minute evening walk around the neighborhood |
| FRIDAY | 1-hour walk around town |
| SATURDAY | 1-hour swim or hike |
| SUNDAY | 1 hour at the dog park |

If necessary, you can break exercise into two sessions per day. You can also add alternatives in case of adverse weather. You can write up a full month in advance, with the weekdays being fairly similar and all the weekends having something different.

Dogs are far better at combining physical and mental exercise than people. That's one of the reasons why they stop and sniff—they're exercising their mind. This is why you can get away with less physical exercise on days with inclement weather. There are plenty of indoor activities that you can do that will tire your dog, although they will rely on you engaging his mind.

## Staying Active Outdoors

When people think of exercising a dog, most of those activities are outside, and they are fairly obvious. The following is a list of a wide range of outdoor activities that can keep your dog happily occupied while you exercise:

- **Walking** — This is the most common activity for people and dogs.

- **Jogging** — Far fewer dogs should jog. For example, for all the reasons discussed earlier, you should never jog with a brachial dog, puppies, older dogs, or most small breeds. If you want to jog with your dog, check with your vet to make sure it is safe.

- **Fetch** — Most dogs love the chase, and fetch is the perfect way to give your dog vigorous exercise without tiring you out. Make sure to use a ball made of real rubber or Frisbees that won't hurt your dog's teeth or mouth.

- **Hiking** — All hikes should end with a check for ticks and other issues.

- **Swimming** — Not all dogs are swimmers, so you must check to see if swimming is a good idea for your pet. Swimming is easy on their joints while also being a real workout. Dogs can swim in pools, but be sure the pool is dog-friendly. Your dog can also swim in rivers, ponds, lakes, and the ocean, but make sure he remains close by at all times, especially in places where there are currents. Usually, you can combine fetch and swimming to keep your dog happily occupied.

- **Biking** — Dogs can join you for a bike ride, but you need to be careful that your dog knows to stay clear of the bike while you are moving. This is only a good activity if you have a high-energy dog who requires more than just a long walk or a jog.

- **Dog sports** — There are many dog sports, such as coursing and agility training. These are usually activities for hardworking dogs who are now pets.

- **Working** — Many mid- to high-energy dogs love being given tasks. They can make fantastic therapy dogs with the right training. You will need to wait until your dog is a bit older and calmer, but as your dog matures, working as a therapy dog can give him the kind of attention that makes up for not being as active. This will require research to determine what requirements and training your dog needs prior to registering him as a therapy dog. You can also have your dog carry things like water bottles during longer exercise. Get creative with ways to put your dog to work. Your dog will love being useful and having a purpose that helps you.

Take all necessary precautions for whatever activities you do so that you can enjoy the time bonding with your dog.

## Staying Active Indoors

If you aren't interested in a sustained exercise session because of a downpour, you can make sure your dog gets the necessary exercise from the comfort of your home. Even large, high-energy dogs can make do with a few days of indoor activity.

Dogs are easy to entertain, and all but the most stubborn ones can enjoy playing indoors.

- Rotate toys (You should have a range of toys, and they should be out of reach of your dog. Storing most of them and having only one or two available at a time means your dog will appreciate those toys much longer. This will make indoor play easier, too).
- Hide-and-seek
- The shell game
- Puzzle toys
- Bubbles
- Food toy
- Indoor fetch
- Careful wrestling
- Training
- Treat hunting (You can do this outside, too.)

Appendix A provides more details on these and other activities to keep your dog happily occupied while tiring him out when you can't play outside.

## The Role of Socialization and Getting Enough for the Day

From fear of the world to aggression to carelessness, it's usually pretty obvious when a dog has not been properly socialized—he simply won't behave well around other dogs and people. Dogs who have been socialized generally feel far less stress, fear, and anxiety.

There is an element of territorial behavior in most dogs, so even the friendliest dogs need to learn that it's all right for people and other dogs to come into their home. To do this, you will need to invite people over to meet your dog. Starting when your dog is still a puppy can make it very easy to socialize your dog with others.

Breeders tend to spend a good bit of time socializing their puppies, so they should have a fairly good baseline when they arrive at your house. If your dog is a rescue, the rescue organization should be able to tell you what they know of the dog's interactions within the facility. The older the dog, the harder it will be to socialize him if this has not been a part of the dog's routine.

A socialized dog will approach the world from a much better place. He will be happier out in public, can enjoy people and dogs when they visit, and won't have a fear that can quickly turn into aggression.

## Socializing Puppies

Puppies will likely enjoy meeting new people, so make sure to invite friends over to help socialize your new canine family member. Your puppy may initially react by barking, but this probably will stop as soon as the person tries to pet your pooch. Still, you will need to be careful to make sure there are no territorial behaviors.

The following is a list of methods to use when introducing your puppy to a new person:

- Try to have your puppy meet new people daily if possible. This could be during walks or while you are doing other activities, both inside and outside of the house. If you can't meet new people daily, try to do so at least four times a week.

- Invite friends and family over and let them spend a few minutes giving the puppy their undivided attention. If your puppy has a favorite game or activity, let people know so they can play with him. This will win the little guy over very quickly and teach him new people are fun and safe to be around.

- Once your puppy is old enough to learn to do tricks (after the first month), have him perform his tricks for visitors.

- Avoid crowds for the first few months. When your puppy is older, attend dog-friendly events so he can learn to be comfortable around large groups of people.

Most dogs will bow and sniff each other during an introduction. Watch for signs of aggression, such as raised hackles and bared teeth. Bowing, high tail, and perked ears usually mean your puppy is excited about meeting the other dog. If your puppy is making noises, make sure the sounds are playful by paying attention to the physical reaction. This applies more if you have adopted an adult, but it's always a good idea to keep an eye out for these signs, regardless of the age of your dog.

The best way to help a puppy feel comfortable around unfamiliar dogs is to set up playdates in a neutral place. This should make the whole experience much easier.

Don't let your puppy jump up on other dogs, no matter how excited he is. This action can become a way of showing dominance, which you don't want with your puppy, even if it is just play in the beginning. If he does jump up, immediately say, "No," to let him know it's not acceptable behavior.

Making friends with people in the neighborhood who have friendly dogs is another way to help socialize your puppy. Not only does it give you people who can easily meet for playdates, but you will also have someone close by to check on your dog if needed. And you can do the same for them.

## Socializing an Adult Dog

There's no guarantee that your dog will be happy being around other dogs. You may be lucky enough to get an adult that is already well-socialized. That doesn't mean you can remain entirely relaxed! Your new dog may have had a terrible experience with a particular breed of dog that no one knows about, and this can result in a bad situation.

Your dog should be adept at the following commands before you work on socialization:

- Sit
- Down
- Stay
- Heel

"Heel" and "Stay" are especially important because they demonstrate that your dog has self-control by remaining in one place based on your command. When you go outside, you will need to be very aware of your surroundings and be able to command your dog before another dog or person gets near you.

- Use a short leash on walks. Being aware of your surroundings will cue you into what makes your dog react so that you can train him not to react negatively.

- Change direction if you notice your canine is not reacting well to a person or dog that is approaching. Avoidance is a good short-term solution until you know your dog is more accepting of the presence of other dogs or people.

- If you are not able to take a different direction, tell your dog to sit, then block his view. This can prove to be challenging, as he will try to look around from behind you. Continue to distract your dog so he will listen to you, taking his mind off what is coming toward him.

- Ask friends with friendly dogs to visit you, then meet in an enclosed space. Having one or two friendly dogs to interact with can help your pet realize not all dogs are dangerous or need to be put in their place. When dogs wander around the area together with no real interaction, your dog will learn that the others are enjoying the outdoors, too. So, there's no reason to try to bully them!

- Get special treats for when you go walking. At the first snarl or sign of aggression, engage the training mentality and draw upon your dog's desire for those special treats. This method is slow, but it's reliable because your dog will learn that the appearance of strangers and other dogs means special treats for him. He will realize going on a walk is a positive experience. Nonetheless, this does not train him to interact with those dogs. Combine this tip with the previous suggestions to get the best results.

If you have ongoing problems with your adult dog, consult a behaviorist or specialized trainer. It might be that you should keep your dog home all the time, in which case you're going to need a big yard to ensure your dog stays healthy. It's never worth the risk of having your dog around other canines if he doesn't like his peers. But an expert may be able to help so that you and your dog don't have to live a hermit-like lifestyle.

## Dog Parks

Dog parks are a mixed bag. You never know how well-trained and socialized dogs are, which makes these parks a bad place to start socializing a puppy. It's best to wait until your dog is older before heading to a dog park.

When your dog is old enough to go to a dog park, make sure to find one that has a good environment.

- Check online reviews about the dog park.
- Talk to your vet.
- Review reports about ailments in the area.

Check the requirements for people to use dog parks. Most of them have certain conditions, such as required shots (something that puppies won't have yet).

Go without your dog the first time. When you get to the park, pay attention to how closely people are watching their dogs. If they are more attentive to other people or their phones, it's best not to go into that kind of environment. Things can go wrong quickly, and distracted pet owners will be much slower to react.

Look around to see if there are dog feces left around the park. If there are, don't stay. Feces attract pests and disease.

When you feel that it's safe, bring your dog. At least for the first few times, go when there are fewer dogs. Early morning or midday tend to be good. Dog parks can be crowded around mid-morning and after work, which can be overwhelming. It's also more likely that the dogs will be hyper and more prone to aggression after a long day sitting at home alone. This can be a bit harder to manage, especially for younger dogs.

Everyone has a bad story about dog parks, but there are also plenty of good stories. Some breeds just shouldn't be at dog parks, such as Dalmatians. Studies have shown that other breeds tend to be more aggressive toward Dalmatians, and it isn't clear why. More important than the breed, though, is how well the dogs have been trained and socialized.

You also need to be aware of the health risks at dog parks. Dogs can collide while running, which can cause bruising and breaks. Your dog may step into a hole. The biggest concern is disease. Like daycare, dog parks are an easy place for illness to spread quickly.

If you decide that dog parks aren't for you and your dog, that is fine. For some dogs, they are a dream come true; for others, it is a bit too much for them. As long as you continue to socialize your dog over the years, it doesn't have to be at a dog park.

# CHAPTER 7

# Training

When it comes to training, your dog's breed is a pretty good predictor for how easy of difficult the task will be. A lot of Retrievers are people pleasers, so they learn quickly. High-energy dogs may be difficult because they could have a hard time focusing if you don't train them right.

Regardless of the type of training, you must be patient and consistent to be successful. Any negative emotions will dissuade your dog from listening, and inconsistent application of the rules will confuse him.

## How All Training Fits into Holistic Care

Basic commands for a dog are similar to basic rules for children. Teaching a dog to sit is similar to teaching a child not to run out in front of traffic; if your dog escapes from you, getting him to sit can keep him from something else that could be detrimental to his health.

Training goes beyond just the physical aspects, though. A dog's training affects nearly every aspect of his life.

A holistic approach means considering the following:

- Your dog's health
- Basic needs
- Personality
- Body language
- Training environment
- Current stress levels
- Normal habits
- Genetics

All of these are relevant to training your dog in a way that is not only effective but in a way that is healthiest for him.

Holistic training is often used to fix bad behavior, such as aggression, destruction, and fear. However, it's the best approach for every dog, whether or not they have problems. Training is essential for dogs because it helps make their lives more structured—something that nearly every dog prefers. Like keeping a schedule, training your dog is part of being a responsible dog parent.

There are many different types of training:

- Basic training
- Potty training
- Puppy training
- Obedience training
- Advanced training
- Tricks/fun training
- Activity training (such as coursing and agility)

All dogs should complete at least the first two types of training (basic and potty training) for their health and happiness. The rest is largely up to your dog's breed, interests, and abilities. A Shih Tzu isn't going to be interested in activity training, and Retrievers don't usually need obedience training.

## Why Training Makes Your Dog Happy

Dogs and children are very similar in what makes them happy, and knowing the boundaries is an essential part of helping them feel safe and secure. Even if you only complete the basics and potty training, it will help your dog feel much more comfortable and happy in your home. Similarly, everyone likes to feel they have a purpose—and that is definitely true for dogs.

Training is how dogs learn the rules and expectations in your home. When they know those rules, they are much more comfortable. The more stubborn breeds may be more than happy to ignore the rules, but that just means they need additional training to keep them from being stubborn in ways that are unsafe. For example, if you train your dog to ignore trash cans, but he goes through your kitchen garbage when you are gone, this can be dangerous.

Most dogs (even a lot of the stubborn ones) will be happy because you are happy when they are successfully trained. All that extra praise and attention is something dogs love. The fact that you respond with positive emotions is a fantastic incentive because dogs are very attuned to our emotions.

## Potty Training

Potty training is necessary to create a comfortable and safe environment for your dog—it's as much about health as it is about training. To be successful, you have to employ a firm, consistent, and understanding approach to encourage your dog. This tends to be more difficult because we want to punish "bad behavior," but in the early days, a dog using the inside of the house to do his business isn't "bad"—it's natural. Consider that humans aren't even able to be potty trained until they can walk, which is usually about two years after they are born. Six months doesn't seem quite so long when you put it in perspective. Keep in mind that your dog isn't misbehaving or intentionally disobeying you; he is learning where to go potty, which is a lot harder than learning how to sit. To speed up the process, be patient and praise your dog when he goes in the right place.

While you are trying to train the dog where to use the bathroom, you will almost certainly see him trying to decide if he should listen to you. All it takes is one time when you allow yourself to be distracted, and you can turn house-training into a

difficult chore. But if you can keep your focus while remaining consistent and firm, most breeds should be trained by six months old.

Staying focused when you have your dog outside for a restroom break isn't necessarily enough; if you fail to keep a constant eye on your puppy when he is exploring inside your home, be prepared for a lot of messes. Puppies will sneak off to use the bathroom inside if you let your attention stray.

This is when learning to be firm and consistent is really going to count, and sticking to the rules will be essential. You will also need to remain calm and patient, as getting upset will only reinforce undesirable behavior. The best tool when house-training a potentially stubborn breed is to set a schedule and stick to it—no deviations! Once your dog realizes you are staying focused and will get him outside for a break, he will accept the rules and do what he's supposed to do.

The following is a list of rules to apply when house-training your puppy:

- Never let the puppy roam the house alone—he should always be in his dedicated puppy space when you're not watching him. No dog wants to spend a lot of time in a soiled crate, so being in his crate is a deterrent from doing his business there when you are not around. He may not feel the same way about other areas of your home if he is free to wander.

- Give your puppy constant, easy access to his designated bathroom spaces with potty pads. You will need to make frequent trips outside with your puppy as he learns where to do his business.

- When you go outside, put a leash on your puppy to make a point of where in the yard you want him to use the bathroom.

- If your puppy doesn't potty within a few minutes, take him inside and put him in the crate for a few minutes. Then, take him back outside to make sure he does go to the bathroom. This isn't punishment for the puppy but a break in case he was getting too distracted to focus on going to the bathroom. Once all stimuli are removed and he's in his crate, he may realize he does have some business to take care of.

Always begin with a training plan; then, be even stricter with yourself than you are with your puppy when keeping to the schedule. You are the key to your puppy's learning.

The following are important considerations when it comes to potty training your puppy:

- Set a schedule.
- Choose a location.
- Establish a key word to signal your dog to go.
- Choose various types of positive reinforcement.

Potty training is something you will have to learn to do, but there are many resources that can help you learn how to train your dog effectively while providing a more holistic approach to this less-than-pleasant job.

# Obedience Training

Obedience training usually includes the following:

- Teaching or reinforcing basic commands, like Sit, Stay, Come, and Down
- How to walk without pulling on the leash
- How to properly greet people and dogs, including not jumping on them

Obedience school helps you learn how to train your puppy while teaching him basic commands and how to behave for basic tasks, like greeting and walking. Classes usually last between seven and 10 weeks.

Ask your vet for recommendations and consider the following when evaluating trainers:

- Are they certified, particularly with the CPDT-KA certification?
- How many years have they been training dogs?
- Do they have experience with training your dog breed?
- Can you participate in the training? If the answer is no, do not use that trainer. You have to be a part of your dog's training because the trainer won't be around for most of your dog's life. Therefore, your dog has to learn to listen to you.
- How clean is the facility?
- How happy are the dogs?

If your dog has anxiety, depression, or other serious behavioral problems, you need to hire a trainer to help your dog work through those issues. Do your research to be sure your trainer is an expert—preferably one with experience training intelligent, strong-willed dogs.

If you have a good bit of experience training dogs, you may be able to train your dog yourself. If you have little to no training, do not attempt this.

Obedience training can be treat-based in the beginning, but it should quickly switch to being praise-based. The goal is to get your dog to learn to listen to you without having to have treats all the time. Praise is better because it's much more cost effective, a better bonding tool, and is best for keeping your dog healthy.

The duration of the training will vary based on your dog's age. Puppies tire quickly, so more than a few minutes isn't going to be effective. The longer a session runs, the

less focused your dog will be, and the more stressed both of you will become. Keep these training sessions productive by keeping them under 15 minutes for mature dogs and under five minutes for puppies. Adjust the training based on your dog's abilities, but do not exceed 15 minutes.

## Fun Training

If you love training your dog and he loves to learn, it will be hard to find an activity that is more rewarding than fun training. Some dogs love to be the center of attention, so fun training gives them the knowledge to really blow away visitors and be the belles of the ball.

Technically, fetch is a game that is a fun training activity. If you've ever tried to play fetch with a puppy or young dog, you know it isn't something that most dogs do naturally. Even if a dog brings the ball or disc back, he may not drop it so that you can throw it again.

Fun training is something you can do inside, giving you another way to exercise your dog indoors. Things like play dead, dance, and beg can use a pretty good bit of energy, as well as be highly entertaining.

The best thing about fun training is that it is a fantastic way to bond with your dog. If you feel yourself starting to get frustrated, stop. If you aren't having fun or your dog is showing signs of disinterest, stop.

There is nearly no limit to the kinds of tricks you and your dog can do. Spend some time going online and watching people train their dogs to do fun tricks, and then see how they trained their dogs. This is the best way to determine what kinds of activities you and your dog may enjoy during fun training.

## Instinct Training

Now, we're getting into the kinds of training that are best for high-energy dogs or dogs with long working histories. Instinct training taps into a dog's natural instincts to encourage those natural behaviors. For example, taking a working dog to a farm or a shepherding dog to a sheep ranch can help him really enjoy what he is drawn to doing. It may be a bit harder for dogs that pull sleds, but there are training sessions for pulling carts and wagons.

The beauty of this type of training is that it focuses on a dog's natural inclinations and fosters those in a way that is healthy for the dog. It encourages a better mental and emotional state, in addition to getting the dog physically active enough to feel better.

To start, many trainers will examine the dog's behavior. From there, they will develop a training plan that focuses on the dog's strengths and interests. Then, they will work with the person and the dog to bring out the best.

This type of training always needs to begin with an expert because the evaluation is what guides the dog's training. Considering that some types of training can be more dangerous, you need an expert to help keep your dog safe.

## Competitive Dog Training

Competitive dog training covers a wide range of activities. Dog shows are a type of competitive dog training, and the focus is on the dog's behavior. Coursing and agility training are often competitive training, too, but the focus is on the dog's natural abilities.

If your dog loves to be active and around other dogs, these activities can be highly engaging and enjoyable for him. Usually, events take hours to full days (or even full weekends) to complete, so it can be a much more time-consuming type of training. However, when it's done, you and your dog will probably be good for a day or two of lower-impact activities while you recover from the experience.

If you want to compete in dog shows, several types of training, particularly obedience training, will be required. It also means being much more aware of how your dog compares to the standards used by the competition. Make sure to do your research first. It's possible that your current dog won't qualify based on the breed standard.

## Boarding Your Dog When You Travel

From a holistic perspective, you should not be vacationing without your dog. Your dog is a member of your family, so it's best to take him with you when you go places. This is better for his mental, emotional, and physical health, especially if he suffers from separation anxiety. If you can't take your dog on vacation, reconsider going.

But there are some types of vacations where you can't bring your dogs, particularly if you're traveling abroad. All nations have quarantine requirements for dogs, and those usually last for longer than you are on vacation.

In the event that your vacation makes it impossible to take your dog, you need to do a lot of research to ensure you are taking care of your dog first. This means looking for boarding when you start your planning process. You should not be looking for a place to board your dog at the last minute.

When you start your search for places to board your dog, begin with sources you trust. Ask the following people who they recommend:

- Your vet
- Your dog trainers
- Friends and family
- Neighbors
- Your dog groomer

With their recommendations in hand, you should

- Look at the reviews online and see if the facility responds appropriately to negative reviews.
- Review their certifications and other qualifications.
- Check any available reports (if available in your area).

Before you commit to a place, go inspect it. You should see how staff act and take care of the dogs and what the facility is like. Before signing up, you should know a lot about how the place operates. This includes:

- How often they feed dogs
- What they feed dogs
- How often the dogs are let out
- If they walk the dogs every day
- How they handle tough situations
- What they will do if your dog falls ill
- How they handle medications
- Their experience with your dog breed

Take the time to think of questions you have before you go check out the facility. You should ask them anything that concerns you. Think about what you would ask if you were hiring a nanny. If you are going to enjoy time away, you need to ensure your dog will be well taken care of while you're gone.

# HEALTH AND WELLNESS

# CHAPTER 8

# Mental and Emotional Health

Your dog's mental and emotional health is just as important as his physical health.

There are some dog breeds that require a certain amount of time alone. Other dogs suffer from separation anxiety, which means leaving them home alone for long periods of time is not a good idea. Some dogs, like Huskies, will make their dissatisfaction known by being incredibly destructive. Other dogs may become increasingly stressed if they're always around people and never given time to themselves. It's a matter of learning your pet's unique needs.

# The Focus of the Holistic Approach

Few things bring more joy than watching a happy dog wag its tail with excitement—it's the kind of moment that fills countless online videos. But dogs don't just express joy; they also show guilt, fear, and uncertainty. A once-wagging tail can tuck between the legs in shame, and a confident stance can turn timid. Just like people, dogs have unique ways of expressing emotions—some wear their feelings on their sleeve, while others remain more reserved and stoic.

To understand your dog's mental state, pay attention to the physical cues. If your dog gets injured and is unable to be as active as he likes, this will have an adverse effect on his mental and emotional state as well. You will notice that he is less energetic and probably more withdrawn. This is a reminder that all parts of your dog's health are connected.

Dogs have the same mental and emotional needs as humans. There are five areas to consider:

- As pack animals, dogs rely on social interactions to be healthy. Leaving a dog home alone for hours at a time is rarely a good idea. If you have to be gone for work, your dog should have a companion so he doesn't get too lonely.

- Some dogs need to feel useful, especially breeds with a long history of being working dogs. Let dogs like German Shepherds and Labs carry water in saddlebags during long walks or hikes. This makes them feel useful. All dogs need some kind of mental stimulation to feel happy; it's just more of a challenge for breeds that have a history of working and need more mental activity than most.

- Allowing your dog to sniff and experience the world around him is important to ensure he gets a mental workout while out of the house. Changing his diet occasionally can also give your dog's brain a workout with different smells and tastes.

- There are many toys and items that can ensure your dog gets regular mental stimulation, even when you aren't actively engaged with him. Activity courses and puzzle toys can keep dogs happily occupied.

- The food your dog eats is just as important for his mental and emotional health as it is to yours. Too much junk food has an adverse effect on your dog's mental health, just like too much sugar can hurt your brain.

It's also important to remember that dogs are very attuned to our feelings. Canines are incredibly empathetic, so when you are feeling down or angry, your dog is going to sense that. There's a good reason why dogs are fantastic emotional support animals.

Your dog's emotions could be a reflection of something you are feeling or at least the way you're emoting around your dog. To help your dog, you may need to do a bit more self-care as well. Do something that both you and your dog will enjoy and that could help both of you feel better mentally and emotionally.

## Mental Stimulation and Health

If you want your dog walks to be more inclined toward exercise, start by going somewhere new and letting your dog sniff for a set amount of time. After that, you can get your exercise in. This warm-up period is good for both of you while also working your dog's mind.

When they don't get enough mental stimulation, a lot of dogs will act out, especially working and intelligent breeds. Often, this is attention-seeking behavior because your dog needs to be doing something. Unlike people, they can't sit and veg—they need to be active both physically and mentally every day. They will be more aware of sounds and smells, which means they are more likely to bark with no obvious source, trying to find their own mental stimulation. They may chew things or run around your home, becoming a bit of a nuisance or even a danger if you have children or elderly people in your home.

This isn't the dog's fault—it's yours.

There are a wealth of toys designed to help keep dogs active. Having other dogs around can help for shorter periods of time, although you want to make sure you don't have two or more dogs who are bored since that will more than likely increase how much trouble they get into.

Appendix B provides some great mentally stimulating activities that you can do inside to keep your dog happy and mentally healthy.

Always rotate out toys. If your dog has constant access to toys, he will lose interest. However, if you put new toys out every week or so, that will be more interesting for your dog, especially at the beginning of the week. Items like Kongs are great because your dog has to work to get the food out, which will keep him entertained for a while.

The best way to keep your dog mentally stimulated, though, is through interactions. Get up a bit earlier and take your dog for a walk somewhere that has interesting smells. The additional mental and physical exercise is much more likely to keep your dog happy for at least a few hours after you head out for work or errands.

## Emotional Health and Stressors

You need to be just as careful with your dog's stress levels as your own. Over time, prolonged stress can cause behavioral issues in your dog.

- Separation anxiety is probably the most well-known type of stress dogs are likely to face. This is something you should know about your dog before you leave him home alone for a long duration. Do trial runs to see how your dog reacts.

- Lack of mental and physical stimulation causes stress, as well as boredom. More intelligent, high- energy, and working dogs are likely to experience this kind of stress.

- Some breeds are particularly sensitive to the emotions of people around them. This can make them more susceptible to feeling stressed if someone is upset around them.

- Dogs may be sensitive to their surroundings. This could mean they don't like a new environment, or it could mean they don't like to be stuck in the same environment day in and day out. You may need to slowly expand your dog's comfort zone or find new places to take him a couple of times a week. Things like hikes are a great way to keep things new for more adventurous dogs.

- If you have to move, the appearance of boxes and other unfamiliar items will upset many dogs.

- Loud noises are another common stressor, such as fireworks and thunderstorms. There are hoods and wraps for dogs to help reduce this type of stress.

- Inconsistent rules can cause a lot of stress in dogs. Like toddlers and teenagers, they are going to test the boundaries, and if it's not clear what they can and can't do, they will feel uncertain. This is why it's critical to always make sure that you're consistent in training your dog and applying the rules. You don't want your dog on edge because he isn't sure what will get him in trouble and what you will let slide simply based on your mood.

All dogs have their own triggers when it comes to stress. Adult dogs are more likely to have stress triggers associated with their past, which can make it more difficult to anticipate potential issues. You need to be aware of your dog's body language and other signs of stress. The next section covers the signs that your dog is feeling stressed and what you should do about it.

## Signs of Stress and How to Alleviate It

There are a lot of potential stressors that may impact your dog's behavior. The following are some of the most typical signs of stress and what you should do to help relieve some of that stress. There is also a section to help you understand strange actions that actually mean your dog is feeling happy — beyond the obvious zoomies!

### General Signs of Stress

Most of the time, the stress your dog feels isn't going to mean he wants space—he's going to want comfort. The following are common signs of stress in dogs:

- Panting and excessive licking
- Cowering, showing more of the whites of his eyes
- Showing teeth and shutting his eyes, almost like a forced smile
- Flattened ears or a furrowed brow
- Tucked tail so that it is down or between the legs
- Loss of appetite
- Inability to sleep much
- Pacing around constantly
- Repeatedly raising his front paw. This could be a bid for attention, but it could also be a way of asking for help
- Whining and whimpering
- Using the bathroom in a place outside the dog's training
- Running or hiding
- Destroying items. (Aggressive chewers may destroy their toys regularly, but this could also be a sign that your dog is stressed.)

With so many potential stressors, you have to pay attention to the environment and monitor your dog to see patterns. Your dog may hear something that you don't, such as thunder in the distance or a fire alarm going off at one of your neighbors' homes.

You know your dog better than anyone, so find out what works to help him relax under different circumstances. Here are some things that may work, depending on what you think is causing the stress and where you are.

- Hats and earmuffs for loud sounds are a good idea. Some dogs may react in fear, and others may get aggressive. Whatever your dog's response, muffling what he hears can help him relax a bit.

- Exercise can help to work out some types of stress, and it's a great distraction.

- Giving your dog some extra attention can help him feel better.

- Head out and have an adventure to get your pup out of a stressful situation.

- Play a game with your dog, such as fetch.

- Play classical music or other calming sounds (such as nature sounds and white noise).

- Grooming or massaging your dog will almost certainly be a welcome way to help him relax.

- Giving your dog shirts and blankets that smell like you so he can surround himself with your scent is an easy way of helping him calm down. There are also special shirts that can help relax a dog.

If your dog is showing signs of stress after a training session, it may be that you're training for too long, your expectations are too high, or you may not be providing positive rein-forcement. All of this can cause extra stress in your dog, as well as ensuring he doesn't learn. Puppies are easy to overtrain, but dogs of any age can become burned out or overstimulated in training. Look for signs that your dog is losing interest. Unless you're training a service animal or working dog, training sessions should be kept to small chunks of time so that your dog enjoys them and learns.

If you have an anxious dog, you may want to consult your vet

about other types of treatment. There are vitamins and supplements, as well as some therapies, that can help. Your vet should know what is available in your area and can make recommendations based on what is likely to work for your dog's unique needs.

Senior dogs will start to lose their vision, memories, and abilities. This will be stressful and frustrating for him. Adjust your life to help keep your dog feeling happy and comfortable. Don't move furniture around, especially if your dog is losing his vision. Keep things as comfortable as possible for him—put down rugs on hard flooring so your dog can walk without losing his balance. Take shorter, slower walks, and let your dog sniff more. He may not be able to be as active as he once was, but he may have more room for mental stimulation. And most dogs will appreciate extra petting and affection as they get older.

## Back Off

Dogs get overwhelmed, so it may be that you need to step back and give your dog space. The following are signs that your dog is telling everyone to back off:

- Growling and snarling are among the most obvious signs that a dog is uncomfortable.

- Exposing teeth in a snarl is a definite indicator that the dog is stressed and needs everyone to move away from him.

- Lowering his body to the ground in a crouched position with his ears laid back means the dog is greatly stressed to the extent that he feels the need to protect his vital organs. It's also a potential pounce/striking position.

- Tucking the tail or holding it straight back so that it's stiff means your dog is not happy.

- Lashing out with nips and snaps at people or animals close by is another clear indicator of a problem.

If you see any of these signs, get everyone to move away from the dog. There are a lot of reasons for a dog to act this way, including overstimulation, having too many people present, or illness or injury.

## Signs Your Dog Is Feeling Great

Knowing when your dog is feeling great is good baseline information to have when you're assessing his stress levels.

Here are the signs that your dog is doing well and feeling happy:

- Open mouth that looks like a smile because the lips aren't pulled back. It doesn't look like your dog is panting unless you have just been active.

- Relaxed body posture, particularly when sleeping.

- Ears are floppy and relaxed.

- Tail is wagging or resting; it doesn't look stiff. Note that some dogs wag their tail as a warning sign. In these cases, their bodies will not be relaxed.

- Bowing and bouncing playfully.

- Leaning into you is a dog's version of a hug.

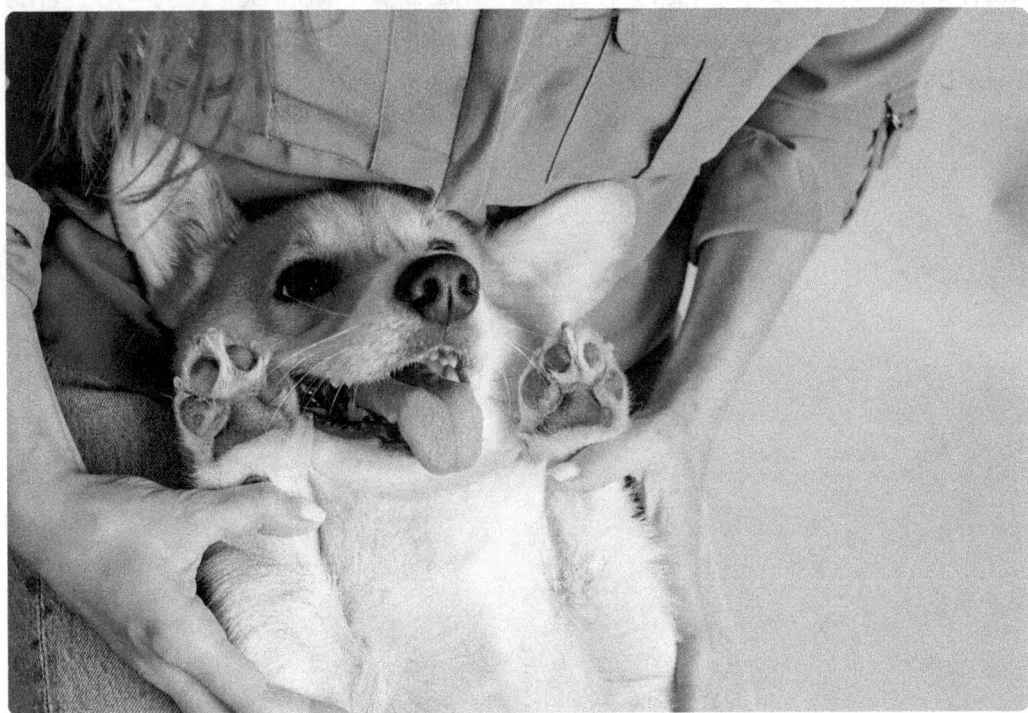

## Leaving a Dog Home Alone

The biggest stressor for most dogs is being left home alone. Even Shiba Inu, a breed notorious for being independent, aren't likely to be happy about being left home alone for a large chunk of the day. Since most people work eight-hour shifts outside of the home, there is probably going to be a large part of the day that is spent away from your dog.

Some dogs can be fine for up to 12 hours on their own, but it's best not to push that if you can help it. If you have a job that requires even longer hours, it's best to get a dog that does better when left alone for longer durations. If you have people who can come by for a few hours to give your dog time and attention, as well as take him out, this can help to remind him he isn't alone.

Having more than one dog is also a good way to ensure your pet isn't alone for long stretches of time. Indoor cameras with voice abilities can let you talk to your dog as well. This can help your dog feel less alone, or it could confuse your dog. Either way, you can see how your dog reacts to determine if it's a good way of keeping your dog company during long stretches alone. If you can stop by home during breaks, this has the added benefit of helping you to relax a bit, too.

After leaving your dog home for a few hours, make sure to spend a bit of time with him once you return. This is probably the highlight of your dog's day—you came back! Even if there's some pouting and guilt-tripping after that initial excitement, enjoy that extra wiggling, wagging, and enthusiasm when you get home. No one can make you feel as welcome as a dog who is really happy to see you.

# CHAPTER 9

# Herbs and Supplements for General Well-Being and Treatment

From providing a good diet and adequate exercise to ensuring your pup has engaging mental stimulation and stress relief, there is a lot you can do to prevent ailments and encourage a healthier life for your dog.

This chapter looks at the things you can do beyond the usual to help your dog be as healthy and happy as possible.

## Preventative Treatments

Preventative treatments can help even the unhealthiest breeds to live their best lives. But some breeds won't be able to handle special treatments, and some won't react well to some supplements. Like his diet, you have to find what works best for your dog.

Keep in mind everything you learned from the previous chapters because all of that will apply here. Monitor your dog's baselines to make sure there aren't any negative effects from the preventative treatments. You want to reduce stress and encourage health.

## Herbal and Supplement Treatments

Herbal therapy has been around nearly as long as people have used plants for medicine. The reason why people still use herbs and plants dozens of millennia later is that they are incredibly effective. They are also far more cost-effective. They are primarily used for the following ailments in dogs:

- To improve their primary systems, such as heart and immune, as well as their kidneys and liver
- To reduce inflammation while improving blood flow
- To help relax muscles
- To help alleviate pain

Herbal therapy should only be used under strict supervision. As long as your dog's health is monitored during this therapy, it's considered safe. However, it can be dangerous if a dog is given the wrong herb or dose of that herb, so never try to administer herbal therapy to your dog on your own.

The following table provides a list of the most common herbs and supplements and their intended effect on dogs, as well as the ailments they can help alleviate.

### Word of Caution

It is always safest to consult your vet before giving any new herb or supplement to your dog. Every breed is different, and every dog within that breed is different. Your vet can help you to know any danger signs to watch for when introducing the them into your dog's diet.

| Herb /Supplement | Common Use | Additional Uses |
| --- | --- | --- |
| Alfalfa | Contains calcium, iron, folate, copper, magnesium, potassium, zinc, and vitamins B1, B12, C, D, E, and K. | Used as an antioxidant to reduce pain and swelling for arthritis. Alfalfa is great for nutritive bone-building or as a diuretic. |
| Aloe vera | When applied to the skin, it can help treat minor injuries, such as scrapes and rashes. | You will need to ensure your dog cannot lick the area where it's applied—aloe vera is poisonous to dogs, so should never be ingested. |
| Anise seeds | Used as an antioxidant to prevent many diseases and are rich in B-complex vitamins and vitamins A and C. | Full of antioxidants and promote many health benefits. |
| Basil (cooking herb) | Boosts the immune system. | |
| Calendula flowers | When applied to the skin, it can help treat minor injuries, such as scrapes and rashes. | It can also be used to treat inflammation, funguses, and bacteria. |
| Chamomile | This can help relax dogs and works as an anti-inflammatory medicine. | It has helped to settle stomachs, as well as rashes and problems on the skin. |
| Ginger | Perfect for your dog's upset stomach. | For breeds with more sensitive stomachs, having ginger treats around can ensure they have something to help settle their tummies a bit. |
| Goldenseal | This is good for treating wounds, particularly around the eyes, as it prevents bacterial infections. | It can help with digestive issues. |

| Herb /Supplement | Common Use | Additional Uses |
| --- | --- | --- |
| Milk thistle | A good supplement when your dog is taking medication that could harm his liver. | |
| Oregano (cooking herb) | Helps upset stomachs. | |
| Peppermint (cooking herb) | Helps upset stomachs. | |
| Rosemary (cooking herb) | A healing herb that can help repair cell damage. | Contains antioxidants, calcium, and other vitamins, so it can help with overall health. |

There are some classifications for common herbs that all have relatively the same effect.

| Category | Herbs | Use |
|---|---|---|
| Apoptogenic | Aralia, ginseng, rhaponticum, rhodiola, schizandra | Used for older dogs to help alleviate stress, improve their mental acuity, and keep their immune system strong. They can also reduce anxiety and improve coordination. |
| Cooking | Basil, oregano, peppermint, rosemary | Small amounts can be mixed in regular food as these have largely general health benefits in addition to specific benefits (previous table). |
| Traditional Chinese herbs | | These herbs are not sold on their own but can be prescribed for a wide range of ailments. |

The following is a list of foods that are good to include in your dog's diet:

- Apples are great for dogs, but only the skin and meat of the fruit. NEVER give your dog the core or the seeds. The rest of the apple can help with digestion.

- Bananas are an excellent source of potassium and vitamins. They're high in sugar, so do not give bananas to your dog often.

- Blueberries are high in antioxidants, and some dogs love them.

- Celery is high in several vitamins, and it can help fight cancer while helping your dog's cardiovascular system.

- Carrots can help with your dog's dental health. It's also entertaining to watch dogs munch down on carrots.

All of these should be given in small amounts as fruits and vegetables are high in sugar (bananas have more than most, so they should be given infrequently).

## Special Vitamins and Compounds

As long as you make sure not to feed your dogs the poisonous foods covered in Chapter 3, many foods you eat can provide vitamins, minerals, and compounds that can help keep your dog healthy.

### Antioxidants

Did you know that antioxidants play a vital role in your dog's health? While some antioxidant-rich foods like dark chocolate are harmful and should never be given to dogs, there are plenty of safe and delicious options your canine companion can enjoy. Blueberries, for instance, are packed with antioxidants and are a favorite treat for many dogs.

Antioxidants protect your dog's cells from damage caused by free radicals. These free radicals are unstable molecules produced during normal bodily processes like digestion and can also result from environmental factors such as exposure to tobacco smoke or natural radiation. Over time, free radicals can cause oxidative stress, leading to cell damage and increasing the risk of chronic diseases like cancer and heart disease.

By incorporating antioxidant-rich foods into your dog's diet, you help neutralize free radicals and support their overall cellular health. In addition to blueberries, strawberries, cranberries, and raspberries are excellent choices that most dogs find appealing. Vegetables like kale, spinach, and carrots are also high in antioxidants and can be added to your dog's meals in moderation.

### Types of Teas — Black and Green

Dogs may not be able to sit down and enjoy a nice cup of tea the way we do, but that doesn't mean they won't also benefit from this popular drink. Black and green teas contain catechins, which have some of the same properties as antioxidants. Green tea is generally considered a better option because it's often caffeine free and has higher levels of catechins.

Talk to your vet before giving your dog either type of tea. Your vet can instruct you on what to do and how to add the tea leaves to your dog's food for the best effect. Your dog shouldn't be drinking tea but can definitely eat properly prepared, dry tea leaves in his food.

## Calcium Supplements

Dogs can benefit from calcium just as much as people. It's good for their bones and can help them stay stronger longer. There are calcium supplements that can be bought over the counter and given to dogs. However, make sure to consult your vet before you do this as these supplements can cause digestive issues for some dogs, including constipation.

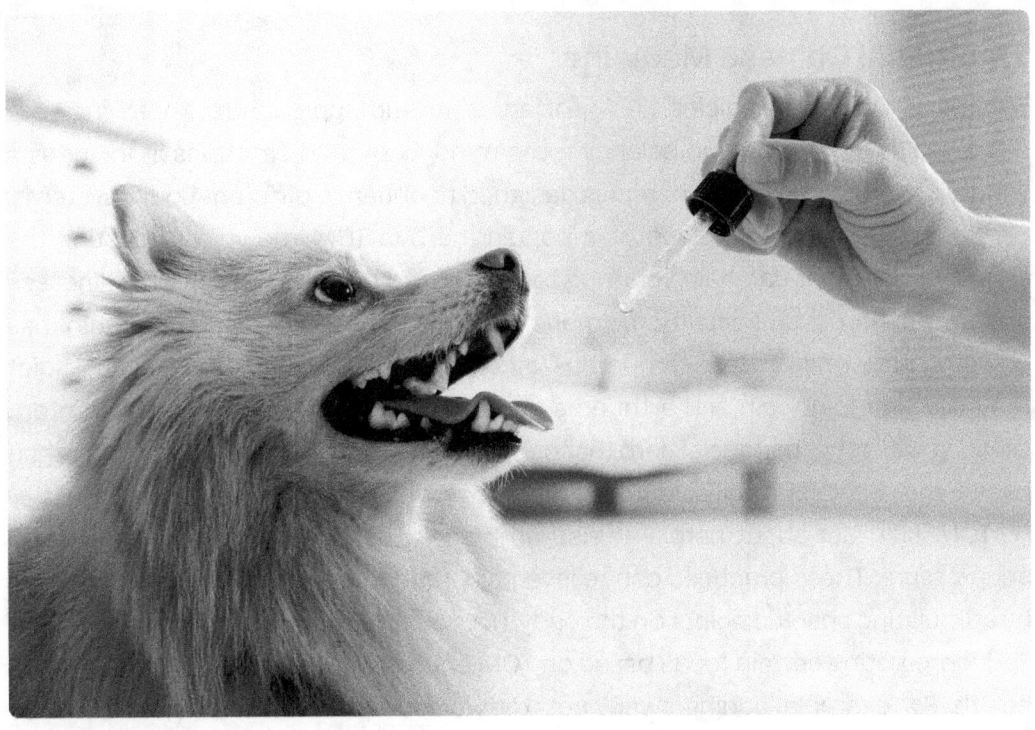

## Calendula

Calendula, also known as pot marigold, is more than just a bright, cheerful flower—it's a fantastic natural remedy for your dog's health. When applied to your pet's skin, calendula acts as a powerful antiseptic and anti-inflammatory agent. This means it can help heal minor wounds, soothe irritated skin, and reduce inflammation. But the benefits don't stop there. Calendula is also high in antioxidants, which, as we mentioned above, play a crucial role in combating free radicals and supporting overall wellness. That's why you'll often find it as a key ingredient in dog supplements. Incorporating calendula into your pet's care routine can contribute to a healthier, happier companion.

## Cetyl Myristoleate

Cetyl Myristoleate is a type of fatty acid that's often used in supplements to help alleviate pain and improve mobility in dogs. Think of it as being similar to omega-3 fatty acids in how it supports joint health. However, some dogs might experience an upset stomach after taking it, so it's important to keep a close eye on your dog's intake and watch for any adverse reactions.

## Traditional Chinese Medicine

Traditional Chinese Medicine (TCM) offers a holistic approach to improving your dog's health by focusing on balancing the mind, body, and emotions. It includes a variety of herbs, foods, and therapies designed to enhance different bodily systems.

For instance, astragalus root is a popular herb in TCM known for boosting the immune system. It can help your dog recover more quickly from chronic illnesses and strengthen overall vitality. Turmeric, with its active ingredient curcumin, has powerful anti-inflammatory properties. Incorporating turmeric into your dog's diet may alleviate joint pain and arthritis symptoms, improving mobility and comfort. Ginseng is another beneficial herb that can enhance energy levels and support organ health, making it especially useful for older dogs who might need an extra boost.

TCM isn't just about herbs—it also embraces therapies like acupuncture and acupressure. These practices can relieve pain, reduce stress, and promote healing by stimulating specific points on the body. (more on this in the next chapter)

Incorporating certain foods based on TCM principles can also support your dog's health. For example, adding sweet potatoes or pumpkin can aid digestion, while green beans can provide essential nutrients without adding many calories.

While these traditional remedies can offer significant benefits, it's important to introduce them thoughtfully. Always consult with a veterinarian experienced in TCM before adding new herbs or therapies to your dog's routine. They can provide guidance tailored to your dog's specific needs, ensuring that any treatments are safe and effective. With the right approach, TCM can be a valuable part of your dog's healthcare regimen, supporting a harmonious balance of mind, body, and spirit.

# CHAPTER 10

# Alternative Therapies

There are many complementary therapies that can be incredibly beneficial for your canine friend. That said, some alternative therapies can cause or exacerbate issues if they aren't done by someone knowledgeable about dogs and their bodies. Always monitor your dog to see what the effects of a treatment are for several rounds before you start regularly trying a therapy for the long term.

## Types of Therapy

You don't need to try all these methods. If something isn't a therapy you would want to do on yourself, it will probably make your dog uncomfortable because he'll sense your discomfort. Only try therapies you feel fully comfortable with.

## Acupuncture

Acupuncture is a cornerstone of traditional Chinese medicine that has been practiced for thousands of years. It involves inserting very thin needles into specific points on the body to stimulate healing and balance. When it comes to our canine companions, acupuncture can offer a gentle and natural way to address a variety of health issues.

### BENEFITS OF CANINE ACUPUNCTURE

**Pain Relief and Inflammation Reduction**

One of the most common uses of acupuncture in dogs is for pain management. Whether your dog is dealing with arthritis, hip dysplasia, or recovering from surgery, acupuncture can help alleviate discomfort. By stimulating the body's natural pain-relieving chemicals like endorphins and serotonin, acupuncture can reduce inflammation and improve mobility.

### Improved Circulation

Enhanced blood flow is another significant benefit. Better circulation means more oxygen and nutrients are delivered to tissues, which can speed up healing and support organ function.

### Neurological Support

For dogs suffering from neurological conditions such as intervertebral disc disease or nerve injuries, acupuncture can stimulate nerve function and aid in recovery. It can help restore mobility and reduce neurological deficits.

### Gastrointestinal Health

Digestive issues like diarrhea, vomiting, or loss of appetite can be distressing. Acupuncture can help regulate gastrointestinal function, easing symptoms and promoting a healthier digestive system.

### Allergy and Skin Conditions

If your dog struggles with allergies or skin problems, acupuncture may help by modulating the immune system and reducing itchiness and inflammation.

### Anxiety and Stress Reduction

Just like humans, dogs can experience anxiety and stress. Acupuncture can have a calming effect on the nervous system, helping dogs who are anxious, fearful, or experiencing behavioral issues.

### Dry Needling

This is the most traditional form, where thin, sterile needles are inserted into specific acupuncture points. It's used to stimulate the body's healing responses.

### Electroacupuncture

In this method, a mild electric current passes between needles. It's especially effective for neurological issues and chronic pain conditions, providing stronger stimulation than needles alone.

### Aqua-Acupuncture

Here, a small amount of sterile fluid (like saline or vitamin solutions) is injected into acupuncture points. The fluid creates pressure, offering prolonged stimulation of the point.

### Laser Acupuncture

For dogs who are sensitive or fearful of needles, low-level laser therapy can stimulate acupuncture points without any penetration of the skin.

### Moxibustion

This technique involves burning a herb called mugwort near the acupuncture points to provide warmth and stimulate circulation. It's beneficial for dogs with conditions aggravated by cold or damp environments.

## INTEGRATING ACUPUNCTURE INTO YOUR DOG'S CARE

Before starting acupuncture, it's crucial to consult with a qualified veterinary acupuncturist. They can assess your dog's specific needs and determine the most appropriate treatment plan. Acupuncture is often used in conjunction with conventional veterinary medicine, supplements, dietary changes, and other holistic therapies.

## WHAT TO EXPECT DURING A SESSION

Most dogs tolerate acupuncture well, and some even relax or fall asleep during the treatment. The needles are very thin, and insertion typically causes minimal discomfort, if any. Sessions can last from 15 minutes to an hour, depending on the treatment plan.

Incorporating acupuncture into your dog's healthcare routine can be a valuable addition to their overall well-being. By addressing a range of physical and emotional issues, acupuncture embodies the holistic philosophy of treating the whole animal.

Always ensure you're working with a certified professional to provide the best care for your furry friend.

Remember, every dog is unique, and what works for one may not work for another. Open communication with your veterinarian and acupuncturist will help tailor the best approach for your dog's specific needs.

## Acupressure

Acupressure is an another ancient healing technique derived from Traditional Chinese Medicine (TCM) that involves applying gentle pressure to specific points on the body. Unlike acupuncture, which uses needles, acupressure relies on touch alone, making it a needle-free and often more comfortable option for dogs—especially those who are anxious or sensitive.

### WHAT IS CANINE ACUPRESSURE?

At its core, acupressure aims to balance the body's energy flow, known as "Qi" (pronounced "chee") in TCM. Practitioners believe that Qi circulates through pathways called meridians. When the flow of Qi is disrupted or unbalanced, it may contribute to various health issues. By stimulating specific acupoints along these meridians, acupressure seeks to restore harmony within the body, supporting natural healing processes.

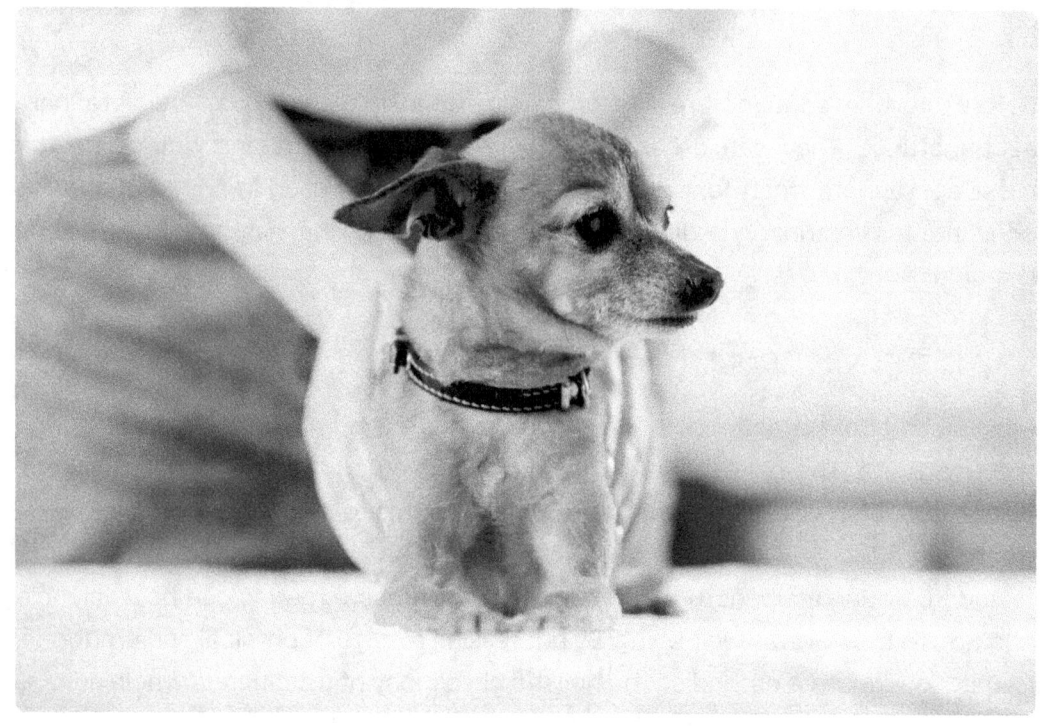

While research on acupressure in animals is still growing, many pet owners and practitioners report several potential benefits:

- **Improved Digestion:** Applying pressure to certain acupoints might help regulate digestive functions, which can be beneficial for dogs experiencing issues like constipation or indigestion.

- **Enhanced Lymphatic Flow:** Stimulating specific points may promote the movement of lymphatic fluids, aiding in detoxification and supporting the immune system.

- **Boosted Immune Function:** Acupressure could help strengthen the body's defenses, potentially reducing the frequency of illnesses.

- **Reduced Anxiety and Stress:** For dogs prone to anxiety, gentle acupressure can have a calming effect, helping them relax during stressful situations like thunderstorms or vet visits.

- **Lowered Blood Pressure:** By promoting relaxation, acupressure may contribute to cardiovascular health, including the regulation of blood pressure.

- **Improved Circulation:** Enhanced blood flow resulting from acupressure can support overall vitality and organ function.

## INCORPORATING ACUPRESSURE INTO HOLISTIC DOG CARE

Acupressure fits seamlessly into a holistic approach by addressing underlying imbalances that may affect your dog's well-being.

For example, if your dog is aging and starting to show signs of arthritis, acupressure can be one component of a comprehensive care plan. Alongside a balanced diet rich in anti-inflammatory nutrients, regular low-impact exercise, and any medications prescribed by your veterinarian, acupressure may help manage pain and maintain mobility.

## LEARNING AND PRACTICING ACUPRESSURE SAFELY

While professional practitioners are trained to locate and stimulate acupoints accurately, you can learn basic acupressure techniques to support your dog's health at home:

- **Use Gentle Pressure:** Always apply light, steady pressure using your fingertips or thumbs. Your dog should remain comfortable and relaxed throughout the session.

- **Observe Your Dog's Responses:** Pay close attention to your dog's body language. Signs of discomfort indicate you should stop or adjust your technique.

- **Integrate into Routine:** Incorporate acupressure into your regular bonding activities, like grooming or petting, to make it a positive experience.

## IMPORTANT CONSIDERATIONS

- **Professional Guidance Is Essential:** Incorrect application of acupressure can potentially cause harm. Learning from a professional ensures you're using safe and effective techniques.

- **Not a Substitute for Veterinary Care:** Acupressure should complement conventional veterinary treatments, not replace them. Always follow your vet's advice regarding medical care.

## AN EXAMPLE ACUPRESSURE POINT

One commonly used point is the "Bai Hui" (Hundred Meetings) point, located on the dorsal midline between the hips at the lumbosacral space. Gently massaging this area can be soothing and is thought to support hind limb strength and alleviate pain associated with arthritis or hip dysplasia. Remember, precise location and technique are important, so consult a professional to guide you.

Adding acupressure to your dog's holistic care plan offers a gentle, non-invasive way to potentially enhance their quality of life. While acupressure isn't a cure-all, it can be a valuable tool when used appropriately and in conjunction with professional veterinary care. As with any new therapy, patience and consistency are key. With proper guidance and a caring touch, acupressure might just become a cherished part of your dog's wellness routine.

## Sound Therapy

Believe it or not, music isn't just for our enjoyment—our dogs can benefit from it too. Sound therapy is an often overlooked but valuable tool in holistic dog care. While it might not be as mainstream as other therapies, incorporating the right sounds into your dog's environment can make a significant difference in their well-being.

Dogs have an incredible sense of hearing, far more acute than ours. This means they're highly sensitive to the sounds around them, which can influence their mood and stress levels. Just as a soothing melody can help us unwind after a long day, the right music can help calm an anxious or overstimulated dog.

One effective way to use sound therapy is by playing calming music during times when your dog might feel stressed. For instance, if your dog gets nervous during thunderstorms or fireworks, having gentle music playing can help mask the scary sounds and provide a sense of comfort. Classical music is often recommended—it has been shown to reduce barking and promote relaxation in dogs. Imagine your pup settling down peacefully to the soothing tones of a Mozart symphony while you're away from home.

Natural sounds can be just as beneficial. The rhythmic ebb and flow of ocean waves or the gentle patter of rain can create a calming backdrop that helps your dog relax. These sounds can also help drown out external noises like traffic or neighborhood activity that might otherwise cause anxiety.

Establishing a routine can amplify the benefits of sound therapy. Playing the same calming music at specific times each day—like during meal times or before bed—can signal to your dog that it's time to relax. Over time, they'll start to associate these sounds with feelings of safety and comfort.

For example, if you have a new puppy adjusting to their home, or an older dog experiencing separation anxiety, consistent use of soothing sounds can ease the transition and reduce stress. It's a simple yet powerful way to enhance their emotional well-being.

While sound therapy isn't as widely used as some other approaches, it's a gentle and accessible method to support your dog's health as part of a holistic care plan. It works beautifully alongside practices like proper nutrition, regular exercise, and social interaction.

Remember, every dog is unique. It might take some experimentation to find the sounds that your furry friend responds to best. Whether it's classical music, nature sounds, or even specially composed pet relaxation tracks, introducing your dog to sound therapy could be a harmonious addition to their care.

# Aromatherapy

Have you ever noticed how your dog responds to different smells? With noses tens of thousands of times more sensitive than ours, dogs experience the world primarily through scent. This incredible sense opens up a valuable avenue for holistic care: aromatherapy. By thoughtfully using specific aromas, we can support our dogs' emotional and physical well-being in gentle, natural ways.

## WHY AROMATHERAPY WORKS FOR DOGS

Aromatherapy taps into the powerful connection between scent and the brain. When dogs inhale certain essential oils, the aromatic compounds interact with their limbic system—the part of the brain that governs emotions and behaviors. This interaction can help alleviate stress, reduce anxiety, and even address physical discomforts. Given their acute sense of smell, dogs can benefit from aromatherapy even at concentrations much lower than what humans use.

## BENEFICIAL AROMAS AND THEIR USES

**Lavender**     Relaxation, anxiety reduction, sleep enhancement

Lavender is renowned for its calming properties. For dogs, it can help ease anxiety during stressful events like thunderstorms or fireworks. A few drops diffused in the air can create a serene environment that helps your pup unwind.

**Chamomile**     Stress relief, digestive support

Chamomile isn't just soothing for humans. Its mild, sweet aroma can help calm nervous dogs and may assist with minor digestive upsets. It's gentle enough for sensitive noses when properly diluted.

**Frankincense**     Immune system support, inflammation reduction

Frankincense has anti-inflammatory and immune-supporting qualities. It can be beneficial for older dogs dealing with arthritis or those recovering from illness. Its warm, grounding scent promotes overall well-being.

**Ginger**     Nausea relief, digestion aid

If your dog gets queasy during car rides, ginger can be a game-changer. Its spicy aroma helps combat nausea and can make travel more comfortable for your canine companion.

**Cedarwood**   Calming effects, natural insect repellent

Cedarwood oil has a soothing effect that can help reduce agitation. Additionally, its natural repellent properties can ward off pests like fleas and ticks, offering a dual benefit.

**Sweet Marjoram**   Muscle relaxation, anxiety reduction

This herbaceous scent helps relax tight muscles and calm the mind. It's particularly useful after vigorous activity or for dogs that have trouble settling down.

## SAFE PRACTICES FOR CANINE AROMATHERAPY

While aromatherapy can be highly beneficial, it's crucial to use it safely:

- **Dilution is Essential:** Always dilute essential oils before use. Dogs are more sensitive to scents, so a concentration that's pleasant to us may be overwhelming for them. A typical guideline is to dilute 1 drop of essential oil in 50 drops of a carrier oil, like coconut or jojoba oil.

- **Use Indirect Inhalation:** Instead of applying oils directly to your dog's skin or fur, use a diffuser in a well-ventilated space. This allows the aroma to disperse gently without overpowering your dog.

- **Monitor Your Dog's Reaction:** Every dog is different. Observe your pet for any signs of discomfort, such as sneezing, whining, pacing, or attempting to leave the area. If you notice any adverse reactions, discontinue use immediately.

- **Avoid Harmful Oils:** Some essential oils are toxic to dogs, including tea tree, eucalyptus, and citrus oils. Always consult with a veterinarian or a certified animal aromatherapist before introducing a new oil.

- **Storage and Safety:** Keep all essential oils and aromatherapy products out of your dog's reach. Curious noses may lead to ingestion, which can be dangerous.

Aromatherapy can be particularly helpful in situations that commonly cause stress or discomfort:

- **During Loud Noises:** Events like thunderstorms, fireworks, or construction can be stressful. Diffusing calming scents beforehand can help your dog stay relaxed.

- **For Separation Anxiety:** If your dog struggles when left alone, soothing aromas can create a more peaceful environment.

- **Post-Exercise or Physical Activity:** Scents that promote muscle relaxation can aid in recovery after hikes, runs, or play sessions.

- **Introducing New Environments:** Moving or traveling can be unsettling. Familiar aromas can provide a sense of comfort in unfamiliar places.

## COMBINING AROMATHERAPY WITH MASSAGE

Enhance the benefits of aromatherapy by pairing it with gentle massage:

- **Relaxation Massage:** Using a diluted blend of lavender or chamomile, gently massage your dog's shoulders, back, and hindquarters to release tension.
- **Joint Support:** For older dogs or those with joint issues, a light massage with diluted frankincense may help ease discomfort.

Always use light pressure and watch your dog's body language to ensure they are comfortable throughout the massage.

Aromatherapy offers a natural, gentle way to support your dog's well-being as part of a holistic care approach. By choosing the right scents and using them safely, you can help alleviate stress, promote relaxation, and enhance your dog's quality of life. Remember, the goal is to complement traditional care—not replace it—and to create a balanced, supportive environment where your dog can thrive.

# Massage

Just like us, our canine companions can benefit immensely from massage therapy. Incorporating massage into your dog's care routine isn't just a luxury—it's a valuable component of holistic health that can improve their quality of life.

Massage therapy for dogs isn't merely about pampering; it's about promoting overall wellness. It can:

- **Relieve Pain and Soreness:** Ideal for aging dogs or those with arthritis, massage can alleviate joint pain and muscle stiffness.

- **Reduce Stress and Anxiety:** Calming touch helps soothe nervous dogs, making it beneficial for those with anxiety or who've experienced trauma.

- **Enhance Circulation:** Improved blood flow aids in healing and boosts energy levels.

- **Strengthen Your Bond:** Spending this quiet, focused time together fosters a deeper connection between you and your pet.

## PROFESSIONAL CANINE MASSAGE THERAPISTS

Taking your dog to a certified professional ensures they're in expert hands. These therapists are trained specifically in canine anatomy and understand how to tailor techniques to your dog's needs.

**Styles Used by Professionals:**

- **Swedish Massage:** Utilizes long, gentle strokes to relax muscles and improve circulation.

- **Trigger Point Therapy:** Targets specific areas of muscle tension, relieving knots and tightness.

- **Myofascial Release:** Focuses on the connective tissue to enhance flexibility and mobility.

- **Acupressure:** Applies pressure to specific points to promote healing and balance energy flow.

**Benefits of Professional Therapy:**

When you opt for professional therapy for your dog, you're accessing a host of benefits that can make a significant difference in their well-being. Professionals have the expertise to spot issues you might miss, such as subtle muscle strains or joint problems. They customize each session to fit your dog's unique health status and temperament, ensuring personalized and effective treatment. Plus, they employ advanced techniques that require in-depth training—methods that go beyond basic care and can greatly enhance your dog's quality of life.

**When to Choose a Professional Therapist:**

- **Health Concerns:** If your dog has specific medical issues, a professional can provide targeted care.

- **Performance Dogs:** Active or working dogs may benefit from specialized muscle recovery techniques.

- **Elderly Pets:** Older dogs often have complex needs that a professional is best equipped to handle.

Alternatively, you might consider learning some massage techniques to use at home. This hands-on approach can be incredibly rewarding for both you and your dog.

**Styles Suitable for At-Home Massage:**

- **Effleurage:** Light, sweeping strokes that warm up muscles and are easy for beginners.
- **Petrissage:** Gentle kneading motions that help relax deeper muscle layers.
- **Passive Touch:** Simply resting your hands on your dog to provide comfort and reassurance.
- **Circular Motions:** Using fingertips to make small circles can relieve tension in specific areas.

**Benefits of DIY Massage:**

One of the great advantages of massaging your dog is the convenience—it can be done anytime, making it easy to incorporate into your regular routine. It's also cost-effective, saving you the expense of frequent professional sessions. Massaging your dog strengthens your relationship, as your canine companion will appreciate the affection and attention. Moreover, regular touch allows you to notice any lumps, bumps, or injuries early on, aiding in prompt detection of potential health issues.

**Tips for Effective At-Home Massage:**

- **Educate Yourself:** Attend workshops, watch tutorials, or read reputable guides on canine massage.
- **Stay Attuned to Your Dog:** Pay attention to their reactions. If they pull away or seem uncomfortable, adjust your technique.
- **Create a Relaxing Environment:** Choose a quiet, comfortable space free from distractions.
- **Be Consistent:** Regular short sessions are more beneficial than sporadic longer ones.

**When DIY Might Not Be Enough:**

- **Complex Health Issues:** Certain conditions require a professional's expertise.

- **Behavioral Challenges:** If your dog is nervous or reactive, a professional can ensure safety and effectiveness.

## FINDING THE RIGHT BALANCE

There's no need to choose one over the other exclusively. In fact, combining both professional and at-home massage can provide comprehensive benefits.

- **Start with a Professional:** Have a therapist assess your dog and perhaps show you some basic techniques.

- **Maintain at Home:** Use what you've learned to continue care between professional sessions.

- **Regular Check-ins:** Periodic visits to a professional can adjust the treatment plan as your dog's needs change.

By embracing massage therapy, you're taking a proactive step in providing the best care for your dog. It's not just about easing aches and pains—it's about enhancing their overall happiness and health. So why not give it a try? Your dog might just thank you with extra tail wags and cuddles.

## Canine Chiropractic Care

Have you ever noticed your dog moving a little stiffly or seeming uncomfortable after a long play session? Just like us, dogs can experience musculoskeletal issues that affect their mobility and overall well-being. That's where canine chiropractic care comes into play as part of a holistic approach to dog care.

Chiropractic care focuses on the alignment of the spine and joints. For dogs, this means that a certified animal chiropractor gently adjusts and manipulates their bones to realign them, particularly along the spine. This realignment can relieve pressure on nerves, reduce pain, and improve mobility. It's especially beneficial for aging dogs who may be dealing with arthritis or general wear and tear on their joints.

If your dog is dealing with certain health issues, canine chiropractic care might offer the relief they need. Here are some conditions where chiropractic adjustments can make a significant difference:

- **Hip Dysplasia:** Common in larger breeds, chiropractic care can help alleviate discomfort and improve joint function for dogs suffering from hip dysplasia.

- **Intervertebral Disc Disease:** Dogs with chronic conditions like intervertebral disc disease may find relief through regular chiropractic adjustments.

- **Injury Recovery:** If your dog is recovering from an injury, chiropractic care can promote healing by ensuring proper alignment and reducing strain on affected areas.

- **Active or Sporting Dogs:** Dogs that participate in agility, flyball, or other high-impact activities can benefit from chiropractic care to maintain optimal alignment and prevent injuries.

- **Arthritis:** Older dogs with arthritis can experience improved mobility and decreased pain through gentle chiropractic manipulations.

- **Muscle Spasms and Tension:** Chiropractic adjustments can relieve muscle spasms and reduce tension, enhancing your dog's overall comfort.

- **Limited Mobility or Stiffness:** Dogs showing signs of stiffness or reduced range of motion may find increased flexibility after chiropractic treatments.

- **Post-Surgical Support:** After surgery, chiropractic care can aid in a smoother recovery by improving circulation and reducing compensatory stress on the body.

- **Behavioral Changes Due to Pain:** If your dog exhibits behavioral changes like irritability or withdrawal, it might be due to underlying pain that chiropractic care can address.

- **Neck and Back Pain:** Just like humans, dogs can suffer from spinal discomfort, and chiropractic adjustments can provide significant relief.

Considering chiropractic care could be a great step toward improving your dog's quality of life. Always consult with a qualified canine chiropractor to see how these treatments can be tailored to your dog's specific needs.

Integrating chiropractic care with regular veterinary treatments, proper nutrition, and exercise forms a comprehensive plan that addresses both the symptoms and root causes of various health issues. It's not about replacing conventional medicine but enhancing your dog's health regimen to promote a better quality of life.

However, it's important to approach this therapy with informed caution. When performed correctly by a qualified professional, chiropractic care can offer significant benefits. On the flip side, if done improperly, it can seriously harm your dog. That's why it's crucial to thoroughly research and choose a reputable canine chiropractor. Look for someone who is fully licensed and has verifiable credentials in animal chiropractic care. Your veterinarian may be able to provide recommendations as well.

Canine chiropractic care can be a valuable component of a holistic approach to your dog's health, particularly for mobility issues and chronic pain relief. By combining it with traditional veterinary care and being mindful of potential risks, you can help ensure your furry friend stays happy and active. Always consult with your veterinarian before starting any new treatment to make the best decision for your dog's specific needs.

# CHAPTER 11

# Holistic Treatment of More Serious Illnesses and Conditions

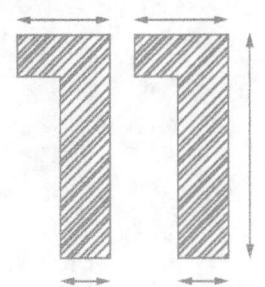

It's best not to make a lot of changes all at once. Trying to do too much will cause your dog stress, probably resulting in an upset stomach. This will make it hard to tell if your dog is having an adverse reaction to a treatment, or if it's just too many changes at one time.

Most of the problems that dogs have with their health can be treated naturally. For example, changing the diet of an overweight dog will also improve his mobility and energy levels. Adjusting an older dog's exercise to fit his abilities will help reduce pain while still keeping the senior pup happy. Adding some extra grooming and massaging for older dogs will also give them a boost to their emotional well-being. That's what is so amazing about a holistic approach—just a few changes can improve your dog's health a great deal.

# Vaccinations

Vaccination schedules are routine for most dog breeds and are an essential part of even holistic and all-natural health care routines. Make sure to add this information to your calendar. Until a puppy has completed his vaccinations, he should avoid contact with other dogs.

The following list can help you schedule your puppy's vaccinations, as well as the regular vaccinations for adult dogs.

| Timeline | Shot |
| --- | --- |
| 6 to 8 weeks | Bordetella, Leptospira, DHPP — First shot<br>Lyme, Influenza Virus-H3N8, Influenza Virus-H3N2 |
| 10 to 12 weeks | Leptospira, DHPP — Second Rabies shot<br>Lyme, Influenza Virus-H3N8, Influenza Virus-H3N2 |
| 14 to 16 weeks | DHPP — Third shot |
| Annually | Leptospira, Bordetella, Rabies<br>Lyme, Influenza Virus-H3N8, Influenza Virus-H3N2 |
| Every 3 years | DHPP Booster, Rabies (if opting for a longer-duration vaccination) |

These shots protect your dog against a range of ailments and should be a part of your dog's annual vet visit so you can continue to keep your pup safe! Note that many places have regulations around vaccines, and nothing discussed in this book is meant to replace those regulations.

# Some Common Ailments

Just like us, our canine friends can suffer from a variety of ailments that range from mildly uncomfortable to downright debilitating. It's tough to watch your dog struggle with issues like persistent skin irritations, digestive problems, or joint pain. These conditions not only affect their well-being but can also impact their happiness and quality of life.

The good news is that holistic approaches offer effective ways to prevent many of these problems, alleviate symptoms when they do arise, and help your dog recover more quickly.

By focusing on the whole animal—mind, body, and spirit—holistic medicine looks beyond just treating symptoms. It aims to address underlying causes and promote overall health. Remember, though, it's essential to consult with your vet if you notice any symptoms. Discuss the holistic treatments you're interested in, and always get a proper diagnosis before starting any new remedies.

## Addison's Disease

This occurs when your dog's adrenal glands are not producing enough aldosterone and cortisol. Aldosterone regulates your dog's electrolytes and water. Cortisol helps your dog deal with stress, which can destroy your dog's immune system and increase the risk of cancer.

The following are symptoms of Addison's disease:

- Dehydration
- Depression
- Diarrhea
- Excessive thirst
- Lethargy
- Poor appetite
- Weakness
- Weight loss
- Vomiting

If you notice these symptoms, take your dog to the vet as soon as possible. If your vet determines that your dog has Addison's disease, oral medication is typically recommended. It's possible that your dog will need to be medicated for the rest of his life. Your vet will monitor your dog to determine if that's necessary. Your dog should be able to resume normal meals and exercise once he starts feeling the effects of the medication.

Additionally, integrating holistic therapies can complement your dog's treatment plan. Providing a balanced, nutrient-rich diet supports adrenal health and overall well-being. Supplements like omega-3 fatty acids, vitamin C, and B vitamins may help strengthen the immune system. Herbal remedies such as licorice root and ashwagandha are believed to support adrenal function. Reducing stress is also crucial—gentle exercise, ample rest, and maintaining a consistent routine can make a significant difference in your dog's recovery. Incorporating calming techniques like massage or the use of dog-safe essential oils might further enhance relaxation and promote healing.

## Allergies

Allergies are a common problem for canines. If you see your dog scratching a lot, there are very good odds that the problem is allergies. Dog allergies are usually a result of allergens (such as dust, mold, or pollen) that irritate the skin or nasal passages. Dogs often develop allergies when they are between one and five years old. Once they develop an allergy, canines never outgrow the problem.

The scientific name for environmental allergies is atopic dermatitis. However, it's difficult to know if the problem is environmental or if it's a food you're feeding your dog.

The following symptoms can be seen when either type of allergy is present:

- Itching/scratching, particularly around the face
- Hot spots
- Ear infections
- Skin infections
- Runny eyes and nose (not as common)

Since the symptoms are the same for food and environmental allergies, your vet will help determine the cause. If your dog has a food allergy, change the food you give him. If he has an environmental allergy, he will need medication, just as humans do. There are several types of medications that can help your dog.

- **Antibacterial/antifungal** — These treatments only address the symptoms that come with allergies; shampoos, pills, and creams usually do not directly treat the allergy itself.

- **Anti-inflammatories** — These are over-the-counter medications that are comparable to allergy medicine for people. Don't give your dog any medication without first consulting with the vet. You will need to monitor your dog to see if he has any adverse effects. If your dog is lethargic, has diarrhea, or shows signs of dehydration, consult your vet immediately.

- **Immunotherapy** — This is a series of shots that can help reduce your dog's sensitivity to whatever he is allergic to. You can learn from your vet how to give your dog these shots at home. Scientists are also developing an oral version of this medication to make it easier to take care of your dog.

- **Topical** — This medication is usually a type of shampoo and conditioner that will remove any allergens from your dog's fur. Giving your dog a warm (not hot) bath can also help relieve itching.

To determine the best treatment for your situation, talk with your vet.

## INHALANT AND ENVIRONMENTAL ALLERGIES

Inhalant allergies are caused by things like dust, pollen, mold, and dog dander. Your dog might scratch at a particular hot spot, or he could paw at his eyes and ears. Some dogs have runny noses and sneeze prolifically, in addition to scratching.

## CONTACT ALLERGIES

Contact allergies mean your dog has touched something that triggers an allergic reaction. Substances like wool, chemicals in a flea treatment, and certain grasses can irritate a dog's skin, even causing discoloration. If left untreated, the allergic reaction can cause the affected area to emit a strong odor or cause fur loss.

Like food allergies, contact allergies are easy to treat because once you know what's irritating your dog's skin, you can remove the problem.

## Anterior Cruciate Ligament Rupture (ACL)

An injury to the leg or knee to the anterior cruciate ligament, better known as the ACL, is something many human athletes have to deal with. When this happens in a big-dog breed, the pain can be extreme. It can cause limping but usually results in the dog being lame. If your dog is overweight, this will exacerbate the problem. When the knee is affected, surgery is required to repair the rupture. Post-surgery, your canine will need to rest between six and eight weeks.

Maintaining a healthy weight is crucial to reduce stress on your dog's joints and ligaments. Incorporating low-impact exercises like swimming or controlled leash walks can strengthen the ACL without overexerting it. Supplements such as glucosamine, chondroitin, and omega-3 fatty acids may also support joint health and improve ligament resilience.

For recovery after an injury, consider holistic therapies like physical rehabilitation to restore mobility and strength. Acupuncture and massage therapy can alleviate pain and promote healing by increasing blood flow to the affected area. Additionally, a diet rich in anti-inflammatory foods and continued supplementation can aid in the recovery process.

## Bladder Stones and Urinary Problems

Uric acid stones can become life-threatening because the stones can block the urinary tract. One of the most common symptoms is that your dog will have trouble urinating, which means little to no urine will come out, even after the dog has been inside for hours. This condition could also cause your dog to have trouble controlling where he urinates, so he has accidents.

Minor cases are treated with medication. More severe cases may require surgery. Diet and medication may also prevent your dog from developing the problem. You can have your dog tested to see if he is prone to stones.

Adding holistic options to your dog's care plan can enhance prevention and promote overall urinary health. Ensuring your dog has constant access to fresh water encourages regular urination, which helps flush out minerals before they form stones. Incorporating a balanced diet with natural, high-quality ingredients and reducing foods high in purines can lessen the risk of uric acid stones. Supplements like cranberry extract and herbs known to support urinary function, such as dandelion root and marshmallow root, might also be beneficial.

## Bloat/Gastric Dilatation and Volvulus (GDV)

Bloat, or Gastric Dilatation and Volvulus (GDV), is a serious condition that mainly affects dog breeds with larger chests. Imagine your dog's stomach filling up with gas—that's bloat. In the worst-case scenario, the gas causes the stomach to twist, preventing anything from entering or leaving. While bloat itself isn't lethal, a twisted stomach can be life-threatening.

Preventing GDV is essential, and there are several steps you can take. Feeding your dog two or three smaller meals a day, instead of one large meal, can make a big difference. Mixing wet dog food with kibble helps reduce the amount of air your dog swallows while eating. And if you opt for dry food, ensure it's rich in calcium.

But beyond these measures, there are holistic supplements and remedies that may help prevent bloat and support overall digestive health:

- **Probiotics and Prebiotics:** These beneficial bacteria promote a healthy gut flora, aiding digestion and reducing gas buildup.

- **Digestive Enzymes:** Supplementing with enzymes can help break down food more effectively, minimizing undigested material that can lead to gas.

- **Herbal Remedies:**

    - **Ginger:** Known for its soothing effects on the stomach, ginger can help reduce nausea and promote healthy digestion.

    - **Fennel:** Fennel can alleviate bloating and gas, making it a helpful addition to your dog's diet.

    - **Chamomile:** This calming herb can soothe the digestive tract and reduce gastrointestinal irritation.

    - **Omega-3 Fatty Acids:** Found in fish oil supplements, omega-3s reduce inflammation in the body, including the digestive system, which can promote better gut health.

In addition to herbal remedies, making some lifestyle changes can significantly reduce your dog's risk of bloat. Here are a few effective strategies to consider:

- **Slow Feeder Bowls:** Using a bowl designed to slow down your dog's eating can prevent them from gulping air, reducing the risk of bloat.

- **Avoiding Vigorous Exercise Around Mealtime:** Ensure your dog isn't engaging in heavy activity immediately before or after eating, as this can contribute to the risk of GDV.

- **Maintain a Calm Eating Environment:** Stress can affect digestion, so providing a peaceful space for your dog to eat can be beneficial.

Remember, while these holistic approaches can support digestive health and potentially reduce the risk of bloat, they shouldn't replace professional veterinary care. Always consult your veterinarian before introducing new supplements or significant changes to your dog's diet. They can provide guidance tailored to your dog's specific needs, ensuring the best possible care for your furry friend.

## Cancer

Cancer is, unfortunately, a common ailment among our canine companions, and its symptoms can vary widely depending on the type and location of the cancer. Some breeds are more susceptible to certain types, which is why researching your dog's breed-specific risks is so important. Early detection is key—it provides the best chance for effective treatment and can significantly improve outcomes.

Let's explore some of the most common cancers found in dogs:

### 1. LYMPHOMA

This cancer affects the lymphatic system, which is vital for immune function. Lymphoma often presents as swollen lymph nodes, but it can impact organs throughout the body.

**Holistic Therapy Options:** Supporting the immune system is crucial. Incorporating antioxidant-rich foods like blueberries and leafy greens into your dog's diet can help. Herbal supplements such as turmeric, known for its anti-inflammatory properties, may also be beneficial. Always ensure any dietary changes are suitable for your dog by consulting with a professional.

### 2. MAST CELL TUMORS

Originating from mast cells involved in allergic responses, these tumors typically appear as skin growths and can vary greatly in appearance and behavior.

**Holistic Therapy Options:** Omega-3 fatty acids from fish oil can support skin health and may reduce inflammation. Additionally, medicinal mushrooms like reishi and maitake are thought to bolster the immune system. Consider natural topical treatments under guidance to soothe the affected area.

### 3. OSTEOSARCOMA

This aggressive bone cancer is most common in large and giant breed dogs, often affecting the limbs and causing significant pain.

**Holistic Therapy Options:** Pain management is vital. Natural anti-inflammatories such as CBD oil (where legal and appropriate) and supplements like glucosamine and chondroitin can support joint health and mobility. Gentle massage and acupuncture may also provide relief and improve quality of life.

## 4. HEMANGIOSARCOMA

A cancer of the blood vessel walls, hemangiosarcoma often develops in the spleen, heart, or skin and is known for its stealthy progression with few early symptoms.

**Holistic Therapy Options:** Strengthening overall health is key. Antioxidant supplements, including vitamins C and E, might support cellular health. Herbs like milk thistle could aid liver function, which is beneficial as the body processes treatments and medications.

## 5. MELANOMA

While commonly associated with skin, in dogs, melanomas frequently occur in the mouth and on the toes. They can be aggressive and may spread quickly to other organs.

**Holistic Therapy Options:** Maintaining oral health is essential. Natural dental care products can help minimize irritation in the mouth. Immune-boosting herbs such as astragalus may support the body's natural defenses.

## 6. MAMMARY GLAND CARCINOMA

Predominantly affecting unspayed females, this cancer forms in the mammary glands and can vary from benign to highly malignant.

**Holistic Therapy Options:** Hormonal balance plays a role here. Dietary additions like flaxseed, which contains lignans, might support hormonal health. Regular gentle exercise can improve overall wellness and aid the body's resilience.

In addition to these specific therapies, there are holistic approaches that can assist with pain relief and mobility across various cancer types. Physical therapies like hydrotherapy allow low-impact exercise, which maintains muscle without overexertion. Acupuncture and acupressure can alleviate discomfort and promote relaxation.

Remember, while these holistic options can support your dog's health and improve quality of life, they should complement conventional veterinary care rather than replace it. It's important to work closely with your veterinarian to develop a comprehensive treatment plan tailored to your dog's specific needs. They can help ensure that any supplements or therapies won't interfere with medical treatments and are safe for your pet.

Early detection and a proactive approach combining traditional and holistic care can make a significant difference in your dog's journey with cancer. Stay observant, keep informed, and don't hesitate to seek professional advice when you notice any changes in your dog's health.

## Copper-Associated Liver Disease

When a dog has too much copper in his liver, it can cause him to appear jaundiced. However, not all dogs actually show any symptoms, which could be a problem. Symptoms are not uniform, so it can be hard to tell when a dog has this issue without having blood work done. As a genetic disease, it is usually screened for in breeds where it is a known issue, such as Labs, Dalmatians, and West Highland Terriers.

Not all dogs have symptoms, so the only way to know they have this disease is to test for it. Other dogs may lose weight, have little to no appetite, act lethargic, frequently vomit, have bouts of diarrhea, or suffer polydipsia. Dogs who have been diagnosed should be treated with supplements and medications.

There are several holistic therapies to support your dog's liver health in the face of copper-associated liver disease. Adjusting your dog's diet to include foods low in copper—like certain poultry, eggs, and white rice—can be a beneficial first step. Supplements such as milk thistle, known for its liver-protective properties, may aid in detoxifying and strengthening liver function. Antioxidants like vitamins E and C can help combat oxidative stress on liver cells, while omega-3 fatty acids from fish oil might reduce inflammation. Remember, it's important to consult with your veterinarian before introducing any new treatments to ensure they're safe and appropriate for your dog's specific needs.

## Deafness

It's estimated that between 15 and 30% of Dalmatians have minor to complete deafness. They are just one of several breeds that tend to be born deaf. In some cases, deafness is a genetic condition. For example, in Dalmatians, the condition is tied to the same thing that causes their gorgeous coat—a reduced production of melanin cells. Melanin is required for normal hearing.

Perhaps the most common reason for deafness is aging, although it's also possible that ear infections or illness can cause a dog to go deaf if left untreated. Since dogs can't tell you when they didn't hear you, and there aren't usually any obvious issues with their ears to let you know, you need to look for signs that your dog may be having issues. The following are some of the symptoms that a dog is losing his hearing:

- Ignoring Calls or Commands: If your dog doesn't come when you call or seems unresponsive to familiar commands, it could be a sign of hearing loss.

- Startling Easily: Dogs that are losing their hearing might be easily startled, especially if they didn't notice you approaching.

- Sleeping More Deeply: A dog with hearing loss may not wake up to noises that would normally rouse them.

- Barking Excessively: Some dogs may bark more than usual because they can't hear themselves bark.

- Not Reacting to Everyday Sounds: If your dog stops responding to sounds like the doorbell, vacuum cleaner, or their favorite squeaky toy, it might indicate a hearing issue.

- Head Shaking or Ear Pawing: Frequent head shaking or scratching at the ears could suggest an ear infection, which can lead to hearing loss if left untreated.

- Difficulty Locating Sounds: Your dog may have trouble finding the source of a sound or might turn the wrong way when you call.

If you've noticed any of these symptoms, it's a good idea to consult your veterinarian. They can determine if your dog is experiencing hearing loss and recommend the best course of action.

## HOLISTIC REMEDIES AND TREATMENTS FOR DEAF DOGS

Living with a deaf dog can present unique challenges, and it's natural to wonder if there's anything you can do to help improve their hearing or enhance their quality of life. While deafness in dogs is often irreversible, exploring holistic and non-traditional methods might offer some support. Let's dive into some alternative approaches that could benefit your furry friend.

### Herbal Remedies and Supplements

Some pet owners have turned to herbal remedies and supplements in hopes of supporting their deaf dogs. Herbs like ginkgo biloba are believed by some to improve circulation and may support nerve health. Similarly, antioxidants found in supplements like vitamin E and vitamin C could contribute to overall ear health. While scientific evidence on their effectiveness for canine deafness is limited, these remedies might offer general health benefits.

### Alternative Communication Methods

Dogs are incredibly adaptable creatures. When one sense diminishes, others often become more pronounced. Incorporating hand signals and visual cues into your training can make communication clear and effective. Consistency is key—ensure everyone in your household uses the same signals. Pairing commands with positive reinforcement, like treats or affection, makes learning enjoyable for your dog.

### Massage and Acupuncture

Physical therapies such as massage can strengthen the bond between you and your dog while promoting relaxation. Some pet owners explore acupuncture as a way to enhance their dog's well-being. Acupuncture involves inserting thin needles into specific points on the body to stimulate healing. While research on its benefits for deafness in dogs is limited, some owners report improvements in their pet's alertness and interaction.

### Proper Nutrition

A balanced diet plays a vital role in your dog's overall health. Ensuring they receive all necessary nutrients can support their well-being. Diets rich in omega-3 fatty acids, for example, have anti-inflammatory properties and may promote neural health. Before making any significant dietary changes or adding supplements, discuss them with your vet to ensure they're suitable for your dog's specific needs.

### Aromatherapy

While scents won't restore hearing, certain aromas might help reduce anxiety and promote relaxation. Lavender, for instance, is known for its calming properties. If you're considering aromatherapy, use pet-safe essential oils and diffuse them in areas where your dog spends time. Remember that dogs have a much stronger sense of smell than humans, so a little goes a long way. Always consult with your veterinarian before introducing new scents, as some oils can be harmful to pets.

### Environmental Enrichment

Enhancing your dog's other senses can help them adapt to hearing loss. Engage their keen sense of smell with scent-based games. Hiding treats around your home or yard encourages them to use their nose to locate goodies. Textured toys and interactive puzzles provide mental stimulation and keep them engaged. Regular physical activity and play are also essential for their emotional and physical health.

### Routine and Structure

Deaf dogs often thrive on routine. Keeping a consistent schedule for meals, walks, and playtime provides a sense of security and helps reduce anxiety. If you need to make changes to their routine, introduce them gradually to give your dog time to adjust comfortably.

**Safety Measures**

Ensuring your deaf dog's safety is paramount. Equip them with a collar and tags that indicate they are deaf. Vibration collars can be a useful tool—not as a punishment, but as a gentle way to get their attention. Always supervise them when outdoors, and in unsecured areas, keep them on a leash since they can't hear potential dangers like approaching cars or other animals.

**Connecting with Professionals and Community**

Don't hesitate to seek guidance from professionals who have experience working with deaf dogs. Animal behaviorists or trainers specializing in hearing-impaired pets can offer valuable techniques tailored to your dog's needs. Additionally, connecting with other owners of deaf dogs through support groups or online communities can provide encouragement and share helpful tips.

While holistic remedies and non-traditional treatments may not restore your dog's hearing, they can significantly enrich their life. With patience, love, and a bit of creativity, you and your deaf dog can navigate this journey together, fostering a deep and rewarding companionship. Remember, every dog is unique, so what works for one might not work for another. Stay observant, be open to trying different approaches, and always keep your dog's best interests at heart.

## Dilated Cardiomyopathy

This is a life-threatening condition where the dog's heart is enlarged, often causing it to have thinner walls. This weakens the heart, which can cause significant issues. There are a number of symptoms associated with this ailment, including the following:

- Heavy breathing when resting or sleeping
- Trouble breathing
- Restless sleep
- Coughing
- Gagging
- Reduced levels of energy
- Fainting
- Decreased appetite
- Weight loss
- Distended belly
- Depressed attitude or lack of interest in interacting

There are a number of tests for the disease, including blood work and EKGs.

Once a dog is diagnosed with the condition, treatment should begin. There are a number of medications that can help to stabilize the problem and then treat it over time. The condition does require aggressive treatment, and there is no guarantee that medications will extend the life of the sufferer. There is no cure.

Now, let's talk about some holistic approaches to support your dog dealing with Dilated Cardiomyopathy. While medications are essential, integrating natural treatments can complement conventional therapy.

- Dietary modifications play a significant role; providing a balanced diet rich in nutrients can help support heart health.

- Supplements like taurine and L-carnitine have shown benefits in some dogs, especially those of breeds prone to deficiencies.

- Incorporating omega-3 fatty acids from fish oil may reduce inflammation and support cardiovascular function.

- Herbal remedies such as hawthorn berry are sometimes used to strengthen the heart muscle. Additionally, managing your dog's stress through gentle exercise and a calm environment can make a difference.

# Epilepsy

Epilepsy is a neurological disorder that causes seizures. The following are signs that your dog may have epilepsy:

- Uncontrollable drooling or foaming
- Biting
- Hackles raised for no obvious reason
- Signs that his vision or hearing is suddenly impaired
- Staring off into space
- Acting hyperactive
- Inability to control his bladder
- Loss of balance
- Tremors
- Seizures, which may include some of the following symptoms:
  - Loss of balance or being unsteady on his feet
  - Collapsing or becoming stiff
  - Going unconscious
  - Shaking and jerking
  - Acting strangely

If your dog starts to have seizures, you need to get him to a vet. Your dog can live a happy, healthy life with early intervention. There are medications that vets will recommend to get seizures under control so that your dog can largely have a normal life. When left untreated, epilepsy can cause brain damage, and in severe cases, it can cause death.

There are some holistic treatment options that might help manage epilepsy in your dog. As always, these should never replace professional veterinary care, they can complement traditional treatments:

- **Dietary Changes:** Adjusting your dog's diet can sometimes reduce seizure frequency. Diets rich in medium-chain triglycerides (MCTs) or ketogenic diets have shown promise in supporting brain health.

- **Herbal Supplements:** Certain herbs like milk thistle, valerian root, and passionflower are believed to support the nervous system. Always consult your vet before introducing any supplements to ensure they're safe for your dog.

- **Acupuncture:** As discussed earlier, this ancient practice can promote overall well-being and may help decrease seizure activity in some dogs by balancing their energy flow.

- **Homeopathy:** Some pet owners find that homeopathic remedies aid in managing epilepsy symptoms. Working with a professional trained in veterinary homeopathy is essential here.

- **Cannabidiol (CBD) Oil:** CBD oil has gained attention for its potential to reduce seizures. Make sure to use products formulated specifically for pets and discuss this option with your vet.

- **Stress Reduction:** Minimizing stress through regular routines, gentle exercise, and creating a calm environment can help prevent seizure triggers.

- **Chiropractic Care:** Adjustments by a qualified animal chiropractor might improve nervous system function and reduce seizure occurrences.

Remember, it's crucial to work closely with your veterinarian when considering these options. They can help tailor a holistic approach that's safe and effective for your dog's unique needs.

## Eye Issues

The following are some of the most common eye problems seen in dogs.

### DISTICHIASIS

"Distichiasis" means "double lashes." As the name indicates, the problem stems from the dog having two full rows of eyelashes on one eyelid. Though it can happen on the upper eyelid, the problem usually occurs on the lower eyelid. In the worst cases it can be all four eyelids, meaning your dog has eight rows of eyelashes that will definitely affect his vision.

It isn't a debilitating condition, but it can cause problems with the cornea and cause excessive tears to form. The vet has several options to treat the condition.

- If the case isn't severe, your dog may not need any treatment.
- For mild cases where the dog is affected, your vet may recommend a lubricant.
- For severe cases, surgery may be needed.

It is not recommended to remove the distichiae since they will grow back, usually thicker. If surgery is needed, it should permanently remove the problem.

There are some holistic approaches that might help manage distichiasis in dogs. While these methods may not eliminate the extra eyelashes, they can alleviate discomfort and support overall eye health.

- Applying warm compresses gently to your dog's eyes can help soothe irritation and promote natural tear production.

- Incorporating omega-3 fatty acids into your dog's diet, through fish oil supplements or foods rich in these nutrients, may also support eye health by reducing inflammation.

- Herbal remedies like eyebright tea (used as a cooled eye wash) have been suggested by some holistic practitioners to ease irritation.

## COLLIE EYE ANOMALY (CEA) AND COLOBOMA

This disease can be mild, with little effect on your dog, but it can also cause blindness. The problem is caused by the dog's eye or eyes not properly forming. In the most severe cases, it can cause holes to develop in layers of the eye, resulting in complete vision loss and retinal detachment.

You can have your dog tested to determine if it's a problem, and if so, it's treatable in most cases. There is no one set of symptoms for this ailment, as each dog can have a different way to compensate for the changes in their vision. That is why testing is essential—you may not have any warning that there is something wrong with your dog. Vets can detect the problem as early as five to eight weeks after the puppy is born. If your vet does find the problem in your dog, there really isn't a treatment or cure. Fortunately, most dogs are minimally affected by CEA. If your dog starts to show signs that his vision is affected, you will need to make adjustments to accommodate his disability.

Another eye illness to watch for is coloboma, which keeps the dog's eye from fully developing. If your dog squints or blinks a lot when you step out in the sun, it could be a sign he has coloboma. This is one of the problems that puppies should be tested for early on so that you can plan to take proper care of your dog if he has the issue. While light sensitivity tends to be the worst problem with coloboma, it's associated with other eye issues, like cataracts. There is no cure for coloboma, but other issues associated with it can be treated. If your dog does have this ailment, try to accommodate for it by avoiding the outdoors when the sun is really bright or sticking to shady areas when you're outside.

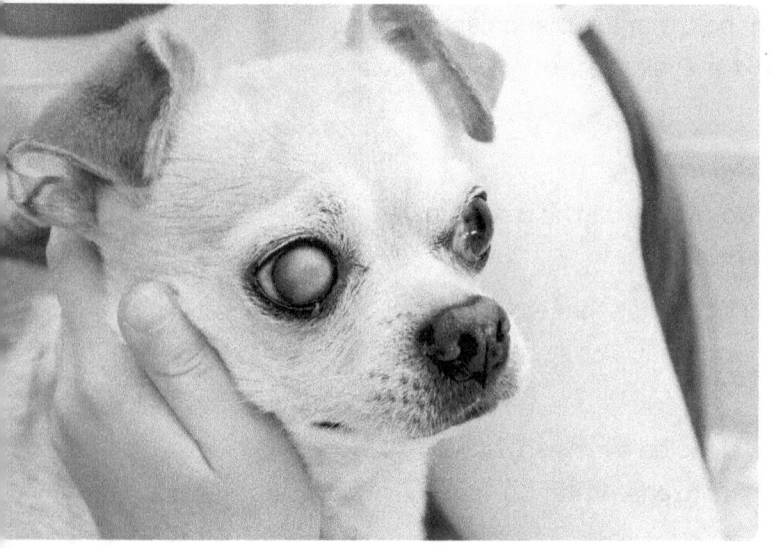

## GLAUCOMA

A painful eye ailment, glaucoma can result in blindness if it isn't treated early. If you notice your dog's eyes watering a lot, squinting, or the cornea turning blue, get him to the vet. These are signs that your dog is in pain.

You can also have your vet do an annual glaucoma screening.

Some holistic options to help prevent and manage glaucoma in dogs include:

- **A diet rich in antioxidants:** Incorporating foods high in antioxidants can support your dog's eye health.

- **Omega-3 fatty acids:** Supplements like fish oil may help reduce inflammation and promote overall eye function.

- **Herbal remedies:** Herbs such as bilberry and ginkgo biloba are believed to enhance ocular health.

- **Acupuncture:** Some pet owners find that acupuncture helps reduce intraocular pressure.

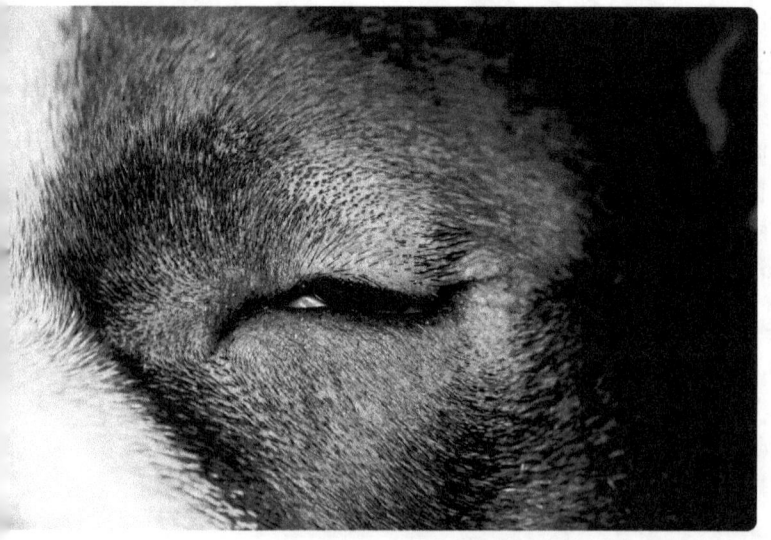

## ENTROPION

Entropion is when the dog's eyelids roll inward, damaging the cornea as the eyelashes scratch it. The corrective surgery that fixes this problem can cause another eye disorder, ectropion. This is when the lower eyelid droops down so you can see the soft pink tissue under the eye. While ectropion is not a serious problem—Basset Hounds live with it as a natural part of their facial structure—it does increase the likelihood of eye infections.

Some holistic options to help prevent and manage Entroion in dogs include:

- **Eye lubrication:** Using preservative-free artificial tears to keep the eyes moist can help reduce irritation caused by the inward-turning eyelids.

- **Warm compresses:** Gently applying warm compresses to the affected eyes may soothe discomfort and decrease inflammation.

- **Reducing environmental irritants:** Minimizing exposure to dust, pollen, and smoke can prevent additional eye irritation that might exacerbate entropion symptoms.

- **Nutritional support:** Incorporating antioxidants and omega-3 fatty acids into your dog's diet may support skin and eye health, potentially aiding in symptom management.

- **Careful grooming:** Keeping the hair around your dog's eyes trimmed can prevent stray hairs from irritating the cornea and worsening the condition.

## IRIS SPHINCTER DYSPLASIA

This medical issue is more commonly found in canines with liver spots but may be found in other dogs at a lower rate. It causes the dog's pupils to look like they are perpetually dilated, which is caused by the muscles around the eyes not working properly. If your dog has this problem, his eyes will be more sensitive to light. It may also make your dog more susceptible to other eye problems.

Treatment is largely based on how severe the case is.

- Simple lifestyle changes that avoid taking your dog into bright lights can help deal with mild cases.

- Homeopathic Solutions: Remedies such as Phosphorus or Gelsemium are sometimes used to address issues with pupil dilation and muscle weakness.

- Vets frequently recommend medications for moderate conditions. The medication will reduce pain and inflammation of the muscles.

- Severe cases often require surgery.

PRA causes sensitivity to light because of problems with the retina. Puppies should be tested for the condition, so if you adopt your puppy from a breeder, you should obtain a guarantee against this particular issue.

Dogs with this condition usually start presenting with night blindness, which can make your dog more nervous in the dark. If you look at your dog's eyes, they may also reflect light more as the eyes deteriorate. The ailment affects both eyes, so the problem should show in both.

While there is no known cure for Progressive Retinal Atrophy (PRA), some pet owners explore holistic therapies that may support their dog's eye health and overall well-being. Here are some options you might consider:

- Antioxidant Supplements: Nutrients like vitamins A, C, and E, along with lutein and zeaxanthin, are thought to support retinal health.

- Omega-3 Fatty Acids: Supplements such as fish oil, rich in omega-3 fatty acids, may promote overall eye health.

- Herbal Remedies: Herbs like bilberry and ginkgo biloba are traditionally used to support vision.

- Acupuncture: Some believe that acupuncture can help manage symptoms by improving circulation and energy flow.

- Dietary Changes: A diet rich in essential nutrients and antioxidants might help support your dog's health.

While these therapies aren't proven to prevent or cure PRA, they might contribute to your dog's quality of life.

# Hemophilia A

This disease affects blood clotting. If a dog has this disorder, a special medication must be applied to any cuts to stop the bleeding. Even small cuts are serious for a dog with Hemophilia A.

Most dogs (and people) who have this problem are likely to suffer from mild anemia. In the worst cases, it can lead to death. The disease can be detected in a blood screening, and any vet will need to know it's a problem to make sure that all possible precautions are taken during a dog's treatment. If your dog has to see a different vet from his usual health-care provider, particularly during an emergency, make sure to let the vet know before any treatment begins. It is recommended that you tell the receptionist so that information is added to the dog's medical record as early as possible.

While Hemophilia A requires medical treatment, incorporating holistic approaches can support overall well-being and complement traditional therapies. Here are some options you might consider:

- **Gentle Physical Activity:** Engaging in low-impact exercises like swimming or walking can help strengthen muscles and improve joint flexibility, potentially reducing the risk of bleeding caused by injuries.

- **Balanced Nutrition:** Maintaining a healthy, nutrient-rich diet supports overall health. While diet alone can't correct the clotting deficiency in Hemophilia A, proper nutrition is important for supporting the body's functions and recovery processes.

- **Stress Management:** Techniques such as meditation, deep-breathing exercises, or yoga may help reduce stress and promote relaxation, which can have a positive impact on your overall health.

- **Physical Therapy:** Working with a physical therapist familiar with Hemophilia A can help you develop exercises to maintain joint health and muscle strength without risking injury.

These holistic strategies can be supportive additions to your comprehensive care plan for Hemophilia A.

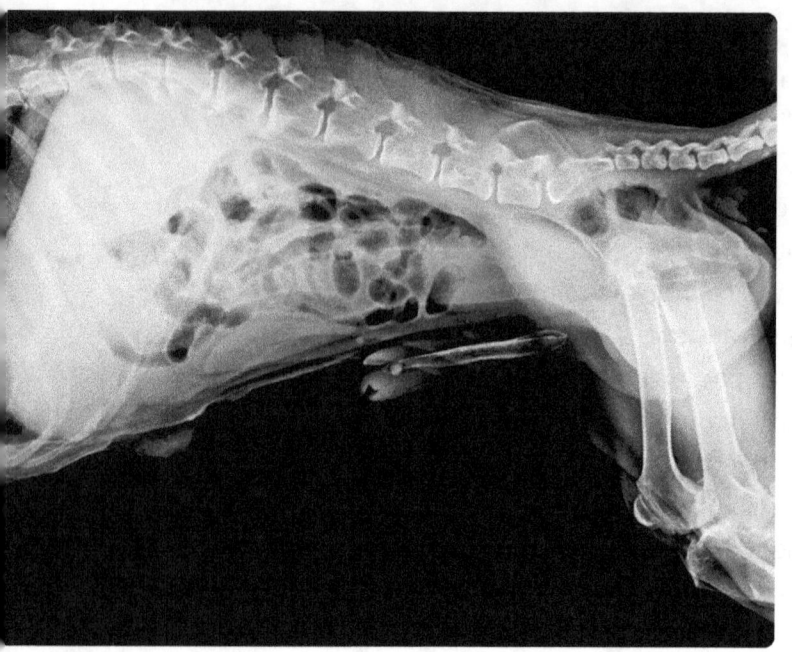

## Hip and Elbow Dysplasia

Hip and elbow dysplasia are common ailments for medium- and larger-sized dogs. Their diet as puppies can help minimize the problem when they are adults. Both types of dysplasia are a result of the dog's hip and leg sockets being malformed, and that often leads to arthritis because the improper fit damages cartilage. The condition can be detected through X-rays by the time a dog becomes an adult.

This is a problem that some dogs try to hide because they don't want to slow down. Your adult dog will walk a little more stiffly or may pant, even when it's not hot. It usually becomes more obvious as a dog nears his golden years. Similar to the way older people change their gait to accommodate pain, your dog may do the same thing.

While surgery is an option in severe cases, most dogs can benefit from less invasive treatment:

- Anti-inflammatory medications — Talk to your vet (dogs should not have large doses of anti-inflammatory drugs on a daily basis, as it can damage their kidneys).

- Lower the amount of high-impact exercise your dog gets, especially on wood floors, tile, concrete, or other hard surfaces. Given how much your dog probably loves to swim, you can move more to a swimming exercise regimen to keep him active without the jarring motions of walking and jogging on hard surfaces.

- Joint fluid modifiers

- Physical therapy

- Weight loss (for dogs who are overweight or obese)

## Hyperthyroid and Hypothyroid

Hypothyroidism is more common than hyperthyroidism, but both conditions are a result of the thyroid producing an incorrect amount of hormones, causing your dog's metabolism to be either too fast (hyperthyroidism) or too slow (hypothyroidism).

If you notice your dog gaining or losing weight without any changes to his food intake and exercise, he may have a thyroid problem. Thyroid disease can also cause your dog to become either more or less hungry. In more severe cases, it can cause vomiting and diarrhea. In some cases, your dog may also grow more or less fur.

Your vet can do a blood test for the condition and will prescribe an oral medication to treat either problem. The medication usually supplements the hormones that the thyroid is not producing or is overproducing.

## Hypertrophic Osteodystrophy

Dogs with hypertrophic osteodystrophy will experience swelling in their bones when they are between four and six months old. The pain and discomfort can cause the dog to be irritable and make it harder for the animal to move. In the most severe cases, dogs may be immobile.

There is no cure for this genetic disease, so treatment is largely geared toward helping you manage your dog's pain. If possible, try to get your dog to relax and be less active when the pain is obvious. There are pain medications that your vet can recommend. If your dog starts to run a high fever, get him to the vet for IV fluid therapy.

Fortunately, as a dog grows, the pain and swelling go away or are greatly reduced and the dog will be able to live a happy, full, active life.

## Legg-Calve-Perthes Disease

Legg-Calve-Perthes is a degenerative bone disease that affects your dog's femurs. Most commonly seen in smaller dogs, it's caused by a disruption to the blood flow, which then weakens the bones. This can result in fractures and scarring of the surrounding tissues. One of the biggest concerns is that it typically leads to arthritis, which makes the problem a long-term concern.

If a dog has this problem, you will notice him limping on the affected leg. Over time, the limping will get worse. Touching the affected leg can be very painful.

Your vet may recommend pain medication. You will also be told to make sure your dog stays in a healthy weight range. Severe cases may require surgery.

## Luxating Patella

Luxating patella is a genetic disease that leads to kneecaps frequently dislocating.

If your dog has this problem, you may notice that he is skipping a step or limping on one leg. In more severe cases, your dog may not use the affected leg at all, meaning he hops around on three legs. When the kneecap slips back into place, your dog will resume a normal gait. As a dog ages, this problem will become worse as other issues present themselves, such as hip or elbow dysplasia or arthritis.

This is a fairly common issue in dogs, so it has been divided into four different classifications of severity.

- Grade I — Any pressure can cause the patella to shift out of place. Once the pressure is removed, the patella goes back in place. No intervention is necessary as it will go back in place on its own.

- Grade II — The patella may pop out of place without any obvious reason. Hyperextending and carefully rotating the leg will move it back into place.

- Grade III — The patella tends to remain out of place, requiring that it be pushed into the groove where it should be.

- Grade IV — The patella will not remain in place, even with manual intervention.

For less severe cases, have your vet show you how to help your dog. For the more severe cases, vets can perform surgery. Most dogs will not require surgery, but you do need to make sure that your dog does not overeat or become overweight, as this will make walking that much harder.

## Multiple Drug Sensitivity (MDS)

Australian Shepherds, in particular, tend to have MDS. This means they're hypersensitive to medications. Even treatments as common as heartworm medication can build up in the dog's brain, causing toxicity.

Puppies should be tested for MDS. If it's determined that a puppy has MDS, you will always need to be cautious about what medications you give your dog.

## Sebaceous Adenitis

This is a genetic skin disease that destroys the sebaceous glands, which produce lubricating secretions. It can cause scales and hair loss. It's a cosmetic problem and isn't life-threatening. Your dog probably won't even notice the problem unless he has another kind of skin infection.

Since the condition is genetic, your vet will need details on the parents in order to test your dog. If that isn't possible, your vet can still run a few tests to try and determine the problem.

If your pup has sebaceous adenitis, the vet will likely suggest a topical or oral therapy to help reduce the effects. More importantly, your dog may need an antibiotic as you likely won't notice the problem in the early days unless there is a secondary infection, which will need to be treated.

## Skin Tumors

It's much easier to detect skin problems in short-haired breeds. If you find lumps on your dog, get him to the vet as soon as possible. It's likely nothing, but you want to make sure the problem isn't something serious.

## Spinal Dysraphism

This is a serious disease that is detectable at birth, so it's not likely that a good breeder will sell a dog with this problem. Dogs that have spinal dysraphism usually have trouble walking because their spinal canal does not properly form. The problem is primarily with their back legs, which means that walking can be incredibly difficult for bigger dogs that have longer spines.

This disease can cause real problems for dogs, and there is no cure, but dogs can still have full lives since it's becoming increasingly easy for vets to provide equipment that can help canines get around with greater ease.

## Subaortic Valvular Stenosis

Subaortic valvular stenosis occurs when an obstruction or lesion forms near the aortic valve. This can cause disruption to the blood flow as it passes through this part of the heart, causing a heart murmur. The problem usually starts to develop when the dog is between three and four weeks old. The condition can be detected in dogs aged six to eight weeks, depending on the severity.

If a dog has a mild-to-moderate case, it likely will not show in a way that makes it easy to diagnose, and the animal will live a life largely unaffected by the disorder. When a dog has a severe case, it's usually coupled with other heart issues, and it will be easier to diagnose through typical means, such as an EKG. It's also more likely to result in the sudden death of the dog if not treated.

Surgery is not effective, but there are medications that can help to manage a severe case. If your dog has this condition, your vet will know he should be given antibiotics before undergoing any type of dental work or surgery.

## Von Willebrand Disease

Von Willebrand disease affects blood platelets by reducing how much protein they receive. It's very serious, and there are no obvious symptoms associated with it. One of the first signs of the disease is if your dog gets a cut and seems to bleed too much for too long.

Like with MDS, dogs with Von Willebrand disease cannot have many typical types of medications, as things like anti-inflammatories and penicillin thin the blood, making the situation worse.

If your dog starts bleeding, get to the vet as quickly as possible. In the event that too much blood is lost, your dog may need a transfusion. Considering the restrictions on your dog, your vet will discuss the best treatment, although taking regular doses of any medication is not recommended.

# Conclusion

Throughout this book, we've delved into the timeless wisdom of holistic care and how it can profoundly enhance your dog's well-being. The principles of a holistic approach aren't new; they're rooted in what humanity has appreciated about the natural world for millennia. While modern veterinary medicine plays a crucial role in treating certain conditions, many of the challenges our dogs face are best addressed through natural, integrated methods.

Caring for your dog holistically means looking beyond mere symptom management. It's about nurturing their physical health, mental stimulation, and emotional balance. Just as you take steps to ensure your own wellness—like eating nutritious foods, engaging in regular exercise, and seeking meaningful connections—the same applies to your canine companion. We've explored how a balanced diet rich in natural ingredients can boost your dog's vitality. We've discussed the importance of regular physical activity not just for their body, but for their mind. And we've highlighted how emotional well-being, fostered through companionship and positive interactions, is essential for a happy dog.

Remember when you feel under the weather? You don't just pop a pill and carry on as if nothing's wrong. You give yourself time to rest, perhaps enjoy comfort foods, or seek the company of loved ones. Your dog deserves the same considerate care. When they're feeling unwell, they benefit immensely from your attention and a comforting environment, alongside any necessary medical treatment.

Embracing a holistic approach doesn't mean disregarding traditional veterinary care. Instead, it's about complementing it—adding layers of natural, preventive, and supportive care that can enhance your dog's quality of life. By integrating holistic practices, you're empowering yourself to take a proactive role in your dog's health journey.

Throughout this book, some key themes have emerged:

- Nutrition is Foundational: Fuel your dog's body with wholesome, natural foods to support their overall health.

- Mind and Body Are Connected: Regular exercise and mental stimulation prevent boredom and promote a joyful disposition.

- Emotional Well-being Matters: Your dog's emotional state affects their physical health. Provide love, security, and companionship.

- Natural Remedies Have Power: Herbs, essential oils, and other natural treatments can support healing and wellness.

- Prevention is Key: Taking steps to maintain health is often more effective than treating illness after it occurs.

Your dog is an incredible companion—loyal, loving, and always ready to brighten your day. By adopting holistic care practices, you're not just addressing issues as they arise; you're investing in a happier, healthier future for your furry friend.

So, as we wrap up our journey together, I encourage you to take these insights to heart. You have the tools and knowledge to make a real difference in your dog's life. Trust your instincts, stay informed, and don't hesitate to blend holistic methods with conventional care.

Remember, caring for your dog holistically is a rewarding endeavor that strengthens the bond between you. It's an approach that honors them as a valued member of your family, deserving of a life filled with health and happiness.

Here's to you and your canine companion—may your journey forward be one of wellness, joy, and many wagging tails.

# Section 5

# PRACTICAL EXTRAS

# Recipes

Your dog is unique, so what he needs is going to vary based on many different factors. His size, build, breed, and activity levels all affect how much he will eat. Your schedule will also affect how many meals you feed him a day. For example, I eat two meals a day, so my dog gets two meals, too.

Keep all this in mind as you make the portion sizes from the recipes. Keep a list of human foods that are safe for dogs. If you eat healthily, it's possible that your food is also acceptable to feed your pup.

Here are some recipes that can help give your dog fresher, healthier options than kibble and canned food.

## Regular Meal

This recipe is for regular meals. You can make large batches of this so you don't have to regularly cook twice a day.

1. Cook one package of boneless ground organic turkey thighs.

2. Add 2 tbsp ground organic organ meat for every 8 oz of ground meat as you cook it.

3. Remove from heat when the meat is pinkish/white.

4. Add the following to a blender.
   a. 1 cup finely grated organic vegetables
   b. 4 tsp ground sunflower seeds

5. Mix the meat and blended vegetables in a bowl.

6. Add the following and stir together:
   a. 2 tsp organic coconut oil
   b. 2 tsp salmon oil

7. Store the food in the refrigerator after giving your dog the recommended amount for his size.

If you would like, you can add the following ingredients to act as supplements to the food:
- 2 g calcium citrate
- 6 tbsp ground foods recommended as supplements (burdock roots, greens, parsley, and zucchini)
- 2 tsp cod liver oil

## Raw Meat Meal

If you want to give your dog a meal of almost all meat, you can occasionally make the following recipe:

Mix the following ingredients in a bowl.

a. 2 lbs ground meat

b. Between 4 and 8 oz raw organ meat

c. 1 cup apple cider vinegar

d. 4 cups blended vegetables

e. 6 eggs (including the shell)

f. 2 tbsp ground kelp

g. 1 cup yogurt

h. A handful of parsley

Store the mixture in the refrigerator until it's gone.

## Simple Chicken and Rice Recipe

If you want to make something really simple, you can regularly make this easy meal for your dog.

1. Boil 2 cups chicken.

2. Cook 1 cup brown rice.

3. Steam 1 cup vegetables.

4. Mix the three ingredients together.

5. Pour 8 tbsp chicken broth over the mixture.

6. Simmer the mixture on low heat for 10 minutes.

You can substitute turkey for chicken, as well as add a bit of dried rosemary (1 tsp) if you want to change up the flavor.

## Simple Beef Stew

Beef is typically one of the cheaper meats. You can cook up a nice stew for your dog with beef during the colder months.

1. Heat 4 tbsp olive oil in a saucepan.

2. Add 2 lbs low-fat beef to the saucepan and cook until the meat is brown.

3. Add 4 pints of beef (or chicken) broth.

4. Simmer the mixture for 45 minutes.

5. Add the following to the stew:
   a. 4 celery sticks (chopped)
   b. 6 carrots
   c. 6 potatoes

6. Stir the food and allow for the vegetables to soften, then cool the meal before you serve it to your dog.

## Healthy Fish Meal

Fish is incredibly healthy, so it would be remiss to exclude it from your dog's diet. You can always add fish oils to the other recipes, but if you want to make something a little more filling and delicious, here's a nice meal to cook up for your dog.

1. Cook 1/2 cup pasta.

2. Add 2 tbsp olive oil to a pan and spread it around.

3. Add 1 salmon steak to the pan and cook it for 5 minutes.

4. Add the pasta to the pan and stir.

5. Add the following to the mixture.
   a. 4 tbsp chicken broth
   b. 1/2 cup steamed vegetables

6. Let simmer for 10 minutes.

Once the food cools, serve it to your very excited dog.

# Indoor Activities

There are many reasons to have indoor activities on hand for your dog. When it's raining, snowing, too hot, too cold, or you're just feeling lazy, you don't want your dog to feel bored. And you definitely don't want him to decide to find his own entertainment!

This chapter provides a lot of ideas for things you can do indoors to keep your dog happy when you want to stay inside.

## Ball Herding

Some breeds love herding, so if that's something in your dog breed's history, you can use that instinct for something incredibly entertaining—ball herding. Take a lot of larger balls, preferably balls that are soft but won't pop, and throw them in different directions, then have your dog herd them into one area.

Create a space on the floor, whether with sturdy pillows or chalk (if you're outside). Show your dog that this is the space where the balls need to be herded, something you can do by having someone else "herd" the balls with you.

1. Have your dog sit in one place and watch you. You, your dog, and the flock of balls should all be within the outlined area in the beginning. Show your dog the flock of balls. You will need to get your dog to remain still when you "release" the flock. Focus on getting your dog to sit still after you throw one ball. Over time, your pup will learn to wait as you release a larger number of balls.

2. Gently roll one or two balls outside of the space, and have your dog fetch them. If your dog plays soccer, he will know how to nudge the balls back into the space a lot easier. Make sure to let your dog know that the space is the "pen" so that he will understand directions for the next couple of steps.

3.  When your dog understands that the flock belongs in the pen (this will probably take a couple of games for your dog to really get the idea), you can finally start with the flock outside of the pen. Have your dog nudge the herd into the pen. With each ball he gets in the pen, give him a treat and a lot of praise. Once all the balls are penned, be incredibly enthusiastic in praising your dog, as canines are not used to "herding" inanimate objects.

4.  When your dog gets adept at the game, start timing him. Make sure that your expectations are realistic based on the length of time it takes your dog to recover the balls. How long you give your pup will likely depend on how many balls you use. This is a game that should be customized to your dog and his abilities. If you start to see frustration, give him more time to complete the task. For example, give him a minute per ball if you have the ball only a couple of feet from the pen. If you start the balls further from the destination, give your dog more time for each ball. As he gets better, you can start reducing the time to challenge your dog.

## Cuddle Time

Younger, more active dogs aren't likely to be fans of cuddling unless they're tired—just like toddlers or small children. But once they get older and settle down, these dogs can be absolutely fantastic cuddlers because they just love being around you. As long as you make sure your dog gets enough exercise, he will be just as happy to relax at the end of the day as you are.

## Dog Fishing

Like fetch, this game doesn't require much energy on your part but can tire your dog pretty quickly. Tie one of the pup's favorite toys to the end of a stick, then drag it around near your dog. You can use an actual fishing rod if you want, but make sure there are no hooks on it. Move the toy over your dog's head, move in circles, or zigzag with it to get your dog to chase it. Occasionally, your dog will "bite," and you can "reel him in" by bringing the toy toward you.

Be careful not to pull too hard once your dog catches the toy.

Make sure to play this game in an open space so your dog doesn't get hurt in all the excitement.

## Indoor Dig

All you have to do is put down pillows, blankets, or towels, and your dog can have his own indoor digging area. Hide a toy or a treat in the middle and watch as your dog throws himself into trying to find what you have hidden. It's easy to set up, and it doesn't take much to hide a toy or another treat again once the first one is located. Your dog does most of the work, and you get to be entertained.

## Hide-and-Seek

Some dogs can get incredibly excited when you try to hide from them. Provide some kind of distraction or ask a family member to hold your dog so you can hide in another room. It isn't going to take long before your dog finds you, but playing the game a few times will be more than enough to get your dog tired.

Once your dog learns all the basic commands, you might be able to get him to sit and stay until you call for him to come find you.

## Ice Cube Escape!

If your dog takes an interest in this game, it can help to cool him down while giving him a way to play without you having to be engaged for most of the playtime. Simply put an ice cube on vinyl (it won't work on carpet or tile), and let your dog try to pick it up. If you have the right-sized cube, this will be a particularly difficult task. Smaller square cubes are best. Half-crescent ice cubes tend to be easier to pick up, so they may not work so well with your canine.

This could result in a bit of clean-up, especially if your dog simply gives up and lets the ice cube melt on the floor. Even if your dog manages to catch and eat the ice, there are good odds there will be water on the floor, as well as a bit of slobber. A small price to pay for the pleasure of seeing your dog having such a great time.

## Laser Pointers

Laser pointers aren't just for cats. Try getting your dog to chase a laser pointer. This may or may not work as your dog may realize that he can't catch it—but if that desire to hunt kicks in, it'll probably be a game you can play for quite some time before your pup wants to do something else. It's a terrific way to expend energy on rainy or chilly days! Being excited yourself can really sell this for your pup to join in the fun.

## Pillow and Blanket Forts

Building a pillow or blanket fort in your home will be a great way to keep your kids and your dog active. They can play hide-and-seek in the fort, crawl around, and generally treat it like their own little castle. Your dog will be very excited about bounding around the fort, giving you a lot of opportunities to take some adorable pictures.

## Puzzle Toys

Puzzle toys are a fun way to get your dog to move around without you having to do much. Most puzzle toys are food-based, so the dog will need to figure out how to get the treats out. Keep in mind any extra calories he consumes playing with these toys.

# Outdoor Activities

When it comes to playing outside, you have a lot of options with your dog. This appendix provides a lot of things you can do to make sure he gets adequate physical and mental exercise every day.

## Agility Training

This is an activity that will tire your dog out both physically and mentally. It isn't an activity for every dog, such as brachycephalic breeds and dogs that aren't particularly athletic. This is something that is designed for active and working dogs who have the necessary stamina and agility.

This is an activity that really helps you bond with your dog, and if you enjoy it, you will have a great outlet for engaging in an activity that reliably tires your dog. Agility training includes a lot of different items, including tunnels, hurdles, cones, teeter-totters, and ramps. You can focus on the activities that your dog really seems to love over time, but you'll want to keep changing up the course because that's what keeps your dog having to think about how best to get through it. To get the most out of each session, the courses should not be predictable.

Before beginning, take your dog to the vet to make sure he is in good physical shape for the activity. This means a complete regular check-up.

There are a number of agility training clubs that can introduce you and your dog to the sport. You can see what kinds of courses they have, learn about recommendations, and see other dogs in action. Over time, you may be able to create your own course at home (you will need a larger yard for this), and then you won't need to travel to run through this fun activity. Still, you should probably continue with the club as a way of having some variety. This will help to keep the sport fun for both you and the dog. It's also a great way to have some built-in socialization time with your dog.

## Beach Time

If you want to go to the beach, your dog will almost certainly love a trip with the family. You will need to make sure that the beach allows dogs. As long as the beach is dog-friendly, you and your dog can enjoy a nice stroll along the sand—it's much easier on paws than concrete or asphalt.

You can play fetch or let your dog enjoy digging on the beach. If you're making sandcastles or want a quick game of Frisbee or keep away, your dog will love to be a part of the games. You can even bury some of his toys and watch your dog enthusiastically retrieve them. It will be easiest if you have plastic toys so that you don't have to spend a lot of time cleaning sand out of the toys when you return home.

If your dog's hair is long, you may not want to take him close to the water. It will be a lot harder for you to groom your dog properly if he has wet hair and a lot of sand gets tangled in it.

## Nose Work

This is another type of training, but it's a bit more specialized than the other commands covered in this book. It's best for your dog to have the other commands down before starting this activity.

To start, get one of your dog's favorite treats or a favorite toy and hide it in a small room or closet. You can also set off a small area of a larger room. To start, your dog should have a pretty limited area so he can get a better idea of what he's supposed to do. Once he finds the treat or toy, give him a reward.

It isn't going to take long for your dog to figure out what you're doing; dogs have spent centuries hunting things down, after all. Once your dog understands, you can start using bigger rooms, or even take the game outside to really give him a workout. You can also graduate to other items; instead of a toy or treat, for example, you can use things like a birch branch.

## Chase

All you have to do to initiate this game is start running away from your dog. The faster you move, the faster your dog will go to stay as close to you as possible. It won't take very long to get your dog tired enough to want to lounge around.

This is a game where you can involve the whole family. If you have kids, you can take the dog and kids out and have them play in the yard, then break out the sprinkler or kiddie pool to cool them down.

If you want to do the pursuing, it's as easy as turning around, throwing your arms in the air, and making a loud noise. Your dog will probably figure out really quickly that he's supposed to turn and run from you. This game often ends with you flopping on the ground and letting your pup lick your face as you laugh.

## Course/Lure Training

Depending on where you live, this may be called either course or lure training. The activity involves your dog chasing after something that is moving quickly. Since dogs have been used as hunters, this gives them some outlet for doing what comes naturally to them—chasing. Unlike hunting, though, the lures are just fake animals that look realistic and move on a mechanism to stay ahead of the dogs. The lures are able to quickly change direction, giving the dogs a real run for their money. You can probably find some lure clubs in your area.

Like agility training, your dog needs to go to the vet to ensure a clean bill of health before starting his activity.

## Give Your Dog a Digging Space of His Own

Your dog will probably want to dig far more often than you'll be able to plant new things in your garden. Instead of trying to have your dog fight a natural desire to dig, play into it and create a digging space just for him.

To create your dog's space, add sand or mulch to an area away from fences or the borders of your home and let your dog do what he loves to do. To encourage your dog to play just in that spot, bury toys, then watch him find them. This will be both mentally stimulating and physically tiring for your dog, so end the game with a nice belly rub session and a bit of peace and quiet.

If it's a rainy or cold day, you can always set up a little pillow fort inside and hide the toy in that. Your dog will have an absolute blast "digging."

## Dog Parks

Dog parks are a great way to socialize your dog, though you will need to be careful in the early days to make sure he enjoys the playtime. Note that if your dog doesn't seem particularly happy being with other dogs, this may not be the best way to spend time outside the home.

If your pet does enjoy dog parks, visiting one several times a week can tire your pupper out. Give him about 30 minutes of playtime, and he'll probably be more than ready to go home. During the summer, plan to go in the early to mid-morning.

## Fetch and Frisbee

You will want to use something soft for this game to avoid hurting your dog's mouth. A soft disc usually runs between $5 and $20, so it won't be a major investment.

All you have to do is throw the disc, and your dog will go get it. Training your dog to bring it back is going to be the trick, but given how much fun this game is likely to be for him, it shouldn't be too hard. Just add "fetch" to your training, and your dog will be more than happy with the results.

Keep in mind it probably won't take long before those discs are slimy when you play. Also, his teeth are probably going to do some damage to the discs. If your dog enjoys the game, it won't hurt to get a stash of discs so that you don't run out of them. When you play, take a couple of discs with you so that you can rotate which one you're throwing to reduce the amount of drool you have to deal with.

## Hiking and Backpacking

If you love being out in nature, some dogs enjoy hiking and backpacking. It depends on the breed and also on the specific dog. Dogs that are brachycephalic (such as pugs), for example, struggle to breathe because of their short snouts and probably aren't the best hiking buddies.

## Homemade Obstacles

If you have a yard, even a small one, you can set up an obstacle course for your dog. A homemade obstacle course can tire out your dog without you having to expend much energy.

- All you need are small orange cones or light plastics to create a weaving obstacle course, and you can train your dog to run around them.

- If you have lightweight, collapsible tunnels, these are perfect for tunnel training. If you don't have them, cardboard boxes can work just as well, and you don't need them to be big to provide a great obstacle course.

- Ramps are easy as well—a few solid planks and cinder blocks are all you need to create a ramp for training. Make sure the ramp is solid and about twice the width of your dog. Don't place any ramp very high off the ground.

If you can create a little maze for your dog, that's even better. Put a treat in the middle of it to really give your dog an incentive.

## Jogging and Biking

Dogs are among the best canine jogging companions. Perhaps the only real downside is that when you're done, your dog may still have some energy to spare. Ending a jogging session with a nice romp through a sprinkler or playing a game of fetch can help burn off the rest of your pup's energy without having to consume a lot more of your own.

If you prefer to ride a bike, you will need to train your dog how to run next to it before taking any long trips, but this probably won't take your dog too long to learn.

## Gardening with Your Dog

Since dogs have a long history of digging, you can help put that instinct to work by letting him help you in the garden. Before doing this, it's essential that your dog be trained in the basics; you don't want him digging in the garden without you around (all gardens should be fenced in as a precaution, with an entrance where you can let the dog walk in with you when you want to work together). You can even have a second garden area just for your dog, and gardening there could be something you do together.

Start by demonstrating where you want to dig and let your pup watch you. It won't take long before your dog will understand what you're doing (at least the digging part) and enthusiastically join you. At this point, you will be able to start monitoring your dog's progress to make sure the holes he digs are deep enough to plant your new flowers, berries, or vegetables. You can even join the dog in digging in the same place so that you have more control over the width of the hole.

When you're done, make good use of the command "Stop," and reward your dog with a treat followed by a grooming session as needed if he's very muddy.

## Joining Earthdog Trials

Dogs often do exceptionally well with Earthdog trials in which they are sent to find a rat located underground or in a den (the rat is in a protective cage, so ethical organizations ensure that no animals are killed during the event). Different courses are created to progressively test a dog's abilities, though it's not a real competition.

If you're interested in enrolling your dog in an event that will tire him out both mentally and physically, this can be a perfect exercise. You can go online and see if there is an organization near you. If so, this can be another great training experience once the basic commands are mastered. If not, the other activities in this chapter will do more than enough to keep your dog happy and (mostly) out of trouble.

## Put Your Dog to Work

With their gregarious, loving nature, a lot of dogs can make great therapy dogs. You will need to wait until your dog is a bit older and calmer before he can start to do this, but as your dog starts to slow down, working as a therapy dog can give him a task that makes up for not being as physically active as he used to be.

You will need to research what requirements and training your dog needs prior to registering him as a therapy dog. It's possible that your dog won't be able to be a therapy dog if he can't meet the requirements. If he does, you'll need to complete any necessary training classes, certifications, or other training before registering your dog.

## Swimming

Before you take your dog swimming, do some research into breed abilities. For example, some dogs are naturally poor swimmers. Other breeds can keep up with you both in the pool or a natural body of water. Most dogs, regardless of breed, do need to be introduced to swimming early in life for them to get the most enjoyment out of it.

Start your dog in pools, ponds, and smaller lakes. Shallower depths can help your dog feel safer faster. Don't worry—you don't have to teach your dog to swim. Any initial apprehension will usually give way to well-honed instincts, and your dog may soon be swimming much faster than any human. Still, stay in the shallower end for at least the first few swims. (And if your dog turns out not to like the water, that's fine. Don't push him.)

If your dog is happy and excited, you can move on to deeper water. Just make sure that you stay close and always keep an eye on your dog. Your dog may overdo swimming in the beginning and then not have enough energy to return. If you go to an ocean or other large body of water, consider a life vest for your dog and also remain vigilant.

There are plenty of different water activities you can do with your pooch. For example, a kiddie pool provides the perfect way to cool down your dog and tire the pooch out with minimal effort on your part. Sprinklers are also a dog favorite.

## Treasure Hunting

In addition to tiring out your canine, treasure hunting can help keep him feeling mentally stimulated.

1. Establish what you want the treasure to be. It should be something that your dog doesn't get often. Treats are usually the go-to because they provide something with a smell the dog will want. You can buy something special, or you can make a treat to really get your dog excited.

2. For the first round, let your dog watch you hide the treat. This is how you introduce him to the idea of you putting something out of sight and that you want him to retrieve it. You will probably need to do this several times, so if you use treats, give him smaller pieces instead of a full, large treat during the learning process. Change where you "hide" the treat so your dog understands that it isn't always hidden in the same place.

3. When you feel that your dog understands what you want him to do, tell your good boy to "Stay" (or if you haven't gotten that far in training, have someone hold your dog), then go hide the treat somewhere your dog can't see you hiding it. Over time, you can hide treats in multiple locations to really challenge your dog's abilities to sniff out the treasure. Then return to your dog and let him go hunting. When he finds a treat, be effusive in your praise.

This is a game you can play inside, though you may want to use dry treats instead of something that could get ground into furniture, carpet, or other items.

## Traveling

A well-trained and well-socialized dog can be one of the best travel companions because he will love being wherever you are. Whether you fly or drive will depend on your particular dog and/or his breed. Either way, your dog will love to see new places, experience new smells, and enjoy the sights and sounds of traveling and camping wherever you go.

Make sure to travel with water so your dog doesn't get dehydrated. If you fly, follow all airline rules for pets. If you drive, ensure the car ride is as comfortable and safe as possible. It's best to have your dog in a crate or secured by a doggy seat belt so he doesn't fall over during sudden stops or turns.

Build in stops for pee breaks, making sure to stop at least every four hours. This will not only give your dog a chance to sniff and enjoy a new place, but you'll also have a chance to stretch your back and legs (which is really better for you, too).

You will want to start traveling when your dog is young, such as taking him to the park, store, or other location. Once your canine is trained in all the basic commands, you can go on longer trips.

## Walking Companion

As long as it isn't too hot or too cold outside, a nice 20- to 30-minute walk around the neighborhood two or three times a day is the perfect daily exercise for you and your dog. Your dog is likely to be bouncy and excited as you stroll around. If there's a nearby park, this will be a great place to go. It isn't likely that your dog will need a frequent change of venue for the walks, making it easier to walk him on a regular basis.

On weekends or trips, you can take hour-long strolls with your dog in new places or even go hiking. Just keep in mind that some dogs have a high prey drive, so plan to keep an eye out for smaller creatures your dog may want to chase.

www.ingramcontent.com/pod-product-compliance
Lightning Source LLC
Chambersburg PA
CBHW081002140626
46546CB00018B/2923